MznLnx

Missing Links Exam Preps

Exam Prep for

Effective Small Business Management

Scarborough, Wilson & Zimmerer, 9th Edition

The MznLnx Exam Prep is your link from the texbook and lecture to your exams.
The MznLnx Exam Preps are unauthorized and comprehensive reviews of your textbooks.

All material provided by MznLnx and Rico Publications (c) 2010
Textbook publishers and textbook authors do not particpate in or contribute to these reviews.

MznLnx

Rico Publications

Exam Prep for Effective Small Business Management
9th Edition
Scarborough, Wilson & Zimmerer

Publisher: Raymond Houge
Assistant Editor: Michael Rouger
Text and Cover Designer: Lisa Buckner
Marketing Manager: Sara Swagger
Project Manager, Editorial Production: Jerry Emerson
Art Director: Vernon Lowerui

Product Manager: Dave Mason
Editorial Assitant: Rachel Guzmanji
Pedagogy: Debra Long
Cover Image: Jim Reed/Getty Images
Text and Cover Printer: City Printing, Inc.
Compositor: Media Mix, Inc.

(c) 2010 Rico Publications
ALL RIGHTS RESERVED. No part of this work covered by the copyright may be reproduced or used in any form or by an means--graphic, electronic, or mechanical, including photocopying, recording, taping, Web distribution, information storage, and retrieval systems, or in any other manner--without the written permission of the publisher.

Printed in the United States
ISBN:

For more information about our products, contact us at:
Dave.Mason@RicoPublications.com

For permission to use material from this text or product, submit a request online to:
Dave.Mason@RicoPublications.com

Contents

CHAPTER 1
Entrepreneurs: The Driving Force Behind Small Business — 1

CHAPTER 2
Strategic Management and the Entrepreneur — 6

CHAPTER 3
Choosing a Form of Ownership — 13

CHAPTER 4
Franchising and the Entrepreneur — 21

CHAPTER 5
Buying an Existing Business — 27

CHAPTER 6
Conducting a Feasibility Analysis and Crafting a Winning Business Plan — 34

CHAPTER 7
Creating a Solid Financial Plan — 41

CHAPTER 8
Managing Cash Flow — 52

CHAPTER 9
Building a Guerrilla Marketing Plan — 58

CHAPTER 10
Creative Use of Advertising and Promotion — 64

CHAPTER 11
Pricing and Credit Strategies — 67

CHAPTER 12
Global Marketing Strategies — 74

CHAPTER 13
E-Commerce and Entrepreneurship — 80

CHAPTER 14
Sources of Equity Financing — 87

CHAPTER 15
Sources of Debt Financing — 93

CHAPTER 16
Location, Layout, and Physical Facilities — 98

CHAPTER 17
Supply Chain Management — 102

CHAPTER 18
Managing Inventory — 110

CHAPTER 19
Staffing and Leading a Growing Company — 114

CHAPTER 20
Management Succession and Risk Management Strategies in the Family Business — 122

Contents (Cont.)

CHAPTER 21
Ethics and Social Responsibility: Doing the Right Thing — 129
CHAPTER 22
The Legal Environment: Business Law and Government Regulation — 134
ANSWER KEY — 144

TO THE STUDENT

COMPREHENSIVE

The *MznLnx* Exam Prep series is designed to help you pass your exams. Editors at MznLnx review your textbooks and then prepare these practice exams to help you master the textbook material. Unlike study guides, workbooks, and practice tests provided by the texbook publisher and textbook authors, *MznLnx* gives you **all** of the material in each chapter in exam form, not just samples, so you can be sure to nail your exam.

MECHANICAL

The MznLnx Exam Prep series creates exams that will help you learn the subject matter as well as test you on your understanding. Each question is designed to help you master the concept. Just working through the exams, you gain an understanding of the subject--its a simple mechanical process that produces success.

INTEGRATED STUDY GUIDE AND REVIEW

MznLnx is not just a set of exams designed to test you, its also a comprehensive review of the subject content. Each exam question is also a review of the concept, making sure that you will get the answer correct without having to go to other sources of material. You learn as you go! Its the easiest way to pass an exam.

HUMOR

Studying can be tedious and dry. MznLnx's instructional design includes moderate humor within the exam questions on occassion, to break the tedium and revitalize the brain

Chapter 1. Entrepreneurs: The Driving Force Behind Small Business

1. An _____ is a person who has possession of an enterprise and assumes significant accountability for the inherent risks and the outcome. It is an ambitious leader who combines land, labor, and capital to create and market new goods or services. The term is a loanword from French and was first defined by the Irish economist Richard Cantillon.
    a. A Stake in the Outcome
    b. Entrepreneur
    c. AAAI
    d. A4e

2. _____ according to Onuoha (2007) is the practice of starting new organizations or revitalizing mature organizations, particularly new businesses generally in response to identified opportunities. _____ is often a difficult undertaking, as a vast majority of new businesses fail. Entrepreneurial activities are substantially different depending on the type of organization that is being started.
    a. A Stake in the Outcome
    b. A4e
    c. AAAI
    d. Entrepreneurship

3. The 'business case for _____', theorizes that in a global marketplace, a company that employs a diverse workforce (both men and women, people of many generations, people from ethnically and racially diverse backgrounds etc.) is better able to understand the demographics of the marketplace it serves and is thus better equipped to thrive in that marketplace than a company that has a more limited range of employee demographics.

    An additional corollary suggests that a company that supports the _____ of its workforce can also improve employee satisfaction, productivity and retention.

    a. Kanban
    b. Virtual team
    c. Trademark
    d. Diversity

4. A _____ is a formal statement of a set of business goals, the reasons why they are believed attainable, and the plan for reaching those goals. It may also contain background information about the organization or team attempting to reach those goals.

    The business goals may be defined for for-profit or for non-profit organizations.

    a. Crisis management
    b. Time management
    c. Business Plan
    d. Distributed management

5. In decision theory and estimation theory, the _____ of an estimator, $\hat{\theta}$, of an unknown parameter of the distribution, θ, is the expected value of the loss function

$$R(\theta, \hat{\theta}) = \mathbb{E}_\theta L(\theta, \hat{\theta}) = \int L(\theta, \hat{\theta})\, dP_\theta.$$

Chapter 1. Entrepreneurs: The Driving Force Behind Small Business

where dP_θ is a probability measure parametrized by θ.

- For a scalar parameter θ and a quadratic loss function,

$$L(\theta, \hat{\theta}) = (\theta - \hat{\theta})^2$$

the _____ function becomes the mean squared error of the estimate,

$$R(\theta, \hat{\theta}) = E_\theta (\theta - \hat{\theta})^2$$

- In density estimation, the unknown parameter is probability density itself. The loss function is typically chosen to be a norm in an appropriate function space. For example, for L^2 norm,

$$L(f, \hat{f}) = \|f - \hat{f}\|_2^2$$

the _____ function becomes the mean integrated squared error

$$R(f, \hat{f}) = E\|f - \hat{f}\|^2$$

a. Linear model
c. Risk aversion

b. Financial modeling
d. Risk

6. _____ describes the situation when output from (or information about the result of) an event or phenomenon in the past will influence the same event/phenomenon in the present or future. When an event is part of a chain of cause-and-effect that forms a circuit or loop, then the event is said to 'feed back' into itself.

_____ is also a synonym for:

- _____ signal; the information about the initial event that is the basis for subsequent modification of the event.
- _____ loop; the causal path that leads from the initial generation of the _____ signal to the subsequent modification of the event.

_____ is a mechanism, process or signal that is looped back to control a system within itself. Such a loop is called a _____ loop.

a. 1990 Clean Air Act
c. Feedback loop

b. Positive feedback
d. Feedback

Chapter 1. Entrepreneurs: The Driving Force Behind Small Business

7. _____, commonly known as e-commerce, consists of the buying and selling of products or services over electronic systems such as the Internet and other computer networks. The amount of trade conducted electronically has grown extraordinarily with widespread Internet usage. The use of commerce is conducted in this way, spurring and drawing on innovations in electronic funds transfer, supply chain management, Internet marketing, online transaction processing, electronic data interchange (EDI), inventory management systems, and automated data collection systems.

   a. Electronic Commerce
   b. Online shopping
   c. A4e
   d. A Stake in the Outcome

8. The term '_____' refers to the concept of collecting information and attempting to spot a pattern in the information. In some fields of study, the term '_____' has more formally-defined meanings.

   In project management _____ is a mathematical technique that uses historical results to predict future outcome.

   a. Least squares
   b. Regression analysis
   c. Stepwise regression
   d. Trend analysis

9. _____ is an integrated communications-based process through which individuals and communities discover that existing and newly-identified needs and wants may be satisfied by the products and services of others.

   _____ is defined by the American _____ Association as the activity, set of institutions, and processes for creating, communicating, delivering, and exchanging offerings that have value for customers, clients, partners, and society at large. The term developed from the original meaning which referred literally to going to market, as in shopping, or going to a market to buy or sell goods or services.

   a. Customer relationship management
   b. Disruptive technology
   c. Market development
   d. Marketing

10. _____ is the state or fact of exclusive rights and control over property, which may be an object, land/real estate or intellectual property. An _____ right is also referred to as title. The concept of _____ has existed for thousands of years and in all cultures.

    a. Emanation of the state
    b. Ownership
    c. A Stake in the Outcome
    d. A4e

11. _____ is an advertisement in which a particular product specifically mentions a competitor by name for the express purpose of showing why the competitor is inferior to the product naming it.

This should not be confused with parody advertisements, where a fictional product is being advertised for the purpose of poking fun at the particular advertisement, nor should it be confused with the use of a coined brand name for the purpose of comparing the product without actually naming an actual competitor. ('Wikipedia tastes better and is less filling than the Encyclopedia Galactica.')

In the 1980s, during what has been referred to as the cola wars, soft-drink manufacturer Pepsi ran a series of advertisements where people, caught on hidden camera, in a blind taste test, chose Pepsi over rival Coca-Cola.

Chapter 1. Entrepreneurs: The Driving Force Behind Small Business

a. 1990 Clean Air Act
b. 33 Strategies of War
c. 28-hour day
d. Comparative advertising

12. A _____ is a business that is privately owned and operated, with a small number of employees and relatively low volume of sales. The legal definition of 'small' often varies by country and industry, but is generally under 100 employees in the United States and under 50 employees in the European Union. In comparison, the definition of mid-sized business by the number of employees is generally under 500 in the U.S. and 250 for the European Union.
   a. Critical Success Factor
   b. Pre-determined overhead rate
   c. Small business
   d. Golden Boot Compensation

13. _____ is a variable work schedule, in contrast to traditional work arrangements requiring employees to work a standard 9am to 5pm day. Under _____, there is typically a core period of the day when employees are expected to be at work (for example, between 11 am and 3pm), while the rest of the working day is 'flexitime', in which employees can choose when they work, subject to achieving total daily, weekly or monthly hours in the region of what the employer expects, and subject to the necessary work being done.

A _____ policy allows staff to determine when they will work, while a flexplace policy allows staff to determine where they will work.

   a. Bennett Amendment
   b. Fiduciary
   c. Certificate of Incorporation
   d. Flextime

14. _____ or _____ data refers to selected population characteristics as used in government, marketing or opinion research, or the _____ profiles used in such research. Note the distinction from the term 'demography' Commonly-used _____s include race, age, income, disabilities, mobility (in terms of travel time to work or number of vehicles available), educational attainment, home ownership, employment status, and even location.
   a. Abraham Harold Maslow
   b. Adam Smith
   c. Affiliation
   d. Demographic

15. The _____ is the Cabinet department of the United States government concerned with promoting economic growth. It was originally created as the _____ and Labor on February 14, 1903. It was subsequently renamed to the Department of Commerce on March 4, 1913, and its bureaus and agencies specializing in labor were transferred to the new Department of Labor.
   a. A4e
   b. A Stake in the Outcome
   c. AAAI
   d. United States Department of Commerce

16. _____, commonly abbreviated to Gen X, is a term used to refer to a generational cohort of children born after the baby boom ended and usually prior to the 1980s

The term _____ has been used in demography, the social sciences, and marketing, though it is most often used in popular culture.

In the U.S. _____ was originally referred to as the 'baby bust' generation because of the drop in the birth rate following the baby boom.

a. Affiliation
b. Abraham Harold Maslow
c. Generation X
d. Adam Smith

17. _____ is a term used to describe the demographic cohort following Generation X. Its members are often referred to as 'Millennials' or 'Echo Boomers') . There are no precise dates for when Gen Y begins and ends. Most commentators use dates from the early 1980s to early 1990s.
    a. Giovanni Agnelli
    b. Benjamin R. Barber
    c. Generation Y
    d. David Wittig

18. _____ is a business management strategy, initially implemented by Motorola, that today enjoys widespread application in many sectors of industry.

_____ seeks to improve the quality of process outputs by identifying and removing the causes of defects (errors) and variation in manufacturing and business processes. It uses a set of quality management methods, including statistical methods, and creates a special infrastructure of people within the organization ('Black Belts' etc.)

    a. Theory of constraints
    b. Six Sigma
    c. Takt time
    d. Production line

19. The _____ is a United States government agency that provides support to small businesses.

The mission of the _____ is 'to maintain and strengthen the nation's economy by enabling the establishment and viability of small businesses and by assisting in the economic recovery of communities after disasters.'

The _____ makes loans directly to businesses and acts as a guarantor on bank loans. In some circumstances it also makes loans to victims of natural disasters, works to get government procurement contracts for small businesses, and assists businesses with management, technical and training issues.

    a. 1990 Clean Air Act
    b. 28-hour day
    c. 33 Strategies of War
    d. Small Business Administration

20. _____ are formal records of the financial activities of a business, person, or other entity. In British English, including United Kingdom company law, _____ are often referred to as accounts, although the term _____ is also used, particularly by accountants.

_____ provide an overview of a business or person's financial condition in both short and long term.

    a. 28-hour day
    b. 33 Strategies of War
    c. Financial statements
    d. 1990 Clean Air Act

Chapter 2. Strategic Management and the Entrepreneur

1. The term _____ collectively refers to all resources that determine the value and the competitiveness of an enterprise. As such, it includes as subsets the attributes that concur to building all financial statements as well as the balance sheet.
   - a. AAAI
   - b. Intellectual capital
   - c. A Stake in the Outcome
   - d. A4e

2. _____ was a writer, management consultant, and self-described 'social ecologist.' Widely considered to be 'the father of modern management,' his 39 books and countless scholarly and popular articles explored how humans are organized across all sectors of society--in business, government and the nonprofit world. His writings have predicted many of the major developments of the late twentieth century, including privatization and decentralization; the rise of Japan to economic world power; the decisive importance of marketing; and the emergence of the information society with its necessity of lifelong learning. In 1959, Drucker coined the term 'knowledge worker' and later in his life considered knowledge work productivity to be the next frontier of management.
   - a. Debora L. Spar
   - b. Chrissie Hynde
   - c. Jacques Al-Salawat Nasruddin Nasser
   - d. Peter Ferdinand Drucker

3. _____ refers to the stock of skills and knowledge embodied in the ability to perform labor so as to produce economic value. It is the skills and knowledge gained by a worker through education and experience. Many early economic theories refer to it simply as labor, one of three factors of production, and consider it to be a fungible resource -- homogeneous and easily interchangeable.
   - a. Deflation
   - b. Productivity management
   - c. Market structure
   - d. Human capital

4. _____ comprises a range of practices used in an organisation to identify, create, represent, distribute and enable adoption of insights and experiences. Such insights and experiences comprise knowledge, either embodied in individuals or embedded in organisational processes or practice.

   An established discipline since 1991, _____ includes courses taught in the fields of business administration, information systems, management, and library and information sciences.
   - a. 28-hour day
   - b. 1990 Clean Air Act
   - c. 33 Strategies of War
   - d. Knowledge Management

5. _____ is, in very basic words, a position a firm occupies against its competitors.

   According to Michael Porter, the three methods for creating a sustainable _____ are through:

   1. Cost leadership

   2. Differentiation

   3. Focus (economics)
   - a. Theory Z
   - b. 1990 Clean Air Act
   - c. 28-hour day
   - d. Competitive advantage

6. _____ is something that a firm can do well and that meets the following three conditions:

Chapter 2. Strategic Management and the Entrepreneur

Competencies are things that companys execute well across several business units or product sectors.

Firms usually have few competencies, but these are usually less liable to change rapidly.

1. It provides consumer benefits
2. It is not easy for competitors to imitate
3. It can be leveraged widely to many products and markets.

A _____ can take various forms, including technical/subject matter know-how, a reliable process and/or close relationships with customers and suppliers (Mascarenhas et al. 1998.)

a. Core competency
c. Learning-by-doing
b. NAIRU
d. Dominant Design

7. Recent strategic thought points ever more clearly towards the conclusion that the critical strategic question is not 'What?,' but 'Why?' The work of Mintzberg and others who draw a distinction between strategic planning (defined as systematic programming of pre-identified strategies) and _____ supports that conclusion. Intensified exploration of strategy from new directions is now coming together in the concept of what is being called _____. At this point, there is no generally accepted definition of the term, no common agreement as to its role or importance, and no standardized list of key competencies of strategic thinkers.

a. Strategic drift
c. Complementors
b. Switching cost
d. Strategic thinking

8. _____ can be regarded as an outcome of mental processes (cognitive process) leading to the selection of a course of action among several alternatives. Every _____ process produces a final choice. The output can be an action or an opinion of choice.

a. 33 Strategies of War
c. Decision making
b. 1990 Clean Air Act
d. 28-hour day

9. _____ is an organization's process of defining its strategy and making decisions on allocating its resources to pursue this strategy, including its capital and people. Various business analysis techniques can be used in _____, including SWOT analysis (Strengths, Weaknesses, Opportunities, and Threats) and PEST analysis (Political, Economic, Social, and Technological analysis) or STEER analysis involving Socio-cultural, Technological, Economic, Ecological, and Regulatory factors and EPISTEL (Environment, Political, Informatic, Social, Technological, Economic and Legal)

_____ is the formal consideration of an organization's future course. All _____ deals with at least one of three key questions:

1. 'What do we do?'
2. 'For whom do we do it?'
3. 'How do we excel?'

In business _____, the third question is better phrased 'How can we beat or avoid competition?'. (Bradford and Duncan, page 1.)

Chapter 2. Strategic Management and the Entrepreneur

a. 33 Strategies of War
b. Strategic planning
c. 1990 Clean Air Act
d. 28-hour day

10. The phrase mergers and _____s refers to the aspect of corporate strategy, corporate finance and management dealing with the buying, selling and combining of different companies that can aid, finance, or help a growing company in a given industry grow rapidly without having to create another business entity.

An _____, also known as a takeover or a buyout, is the buying of one company (the 'target') by another. An _____ may be friendly or hostile.

a. A4e
b. A Stake in the Outcome
c. Acquisition
d. AAAI

11. A _____ is a brief written statement of the purpose of a company or organization. Ideally, a _____ guides the actions of the organization, spells out its overall goal, provides a sense of direction, and guides decision making for all levels of management.

_____s often contain the following:

- Purpose and aim of the organization
- The organization's primary stakeholders: clients, stockholders, etc.
- Responsibilities of the organization toward these stakeholders
- Products and services offered

In developing a _____:

- Encourage as much input as feasible from employees, volunteers, and other stakeholders
- Publicize it broadly

The _____ can be used to resolve differences between business stakeholders. Stakeholders include: employees including managers and executives, stockholders, board of directors, customers, suppliers, distributors, creditors, governments (local, state, federal, etc.), unions, competitors, NGO's, and the general public.

a. 1990 Clean Air Act
b. 28-hour day
c. 33 Strategies of War
d. Mission statement

12. _____, commonly known as e-commerce, consists of the buying and selling of products or services over electronic systems such as the Internet and other computer networks. The amount of trade conducted electronically has grown extraordinarily with widespread Internet usage. The use of commerce is conducted in this way, spurring and drawing on innovations in electronic funds transfer, supply chain management, Internet marketing, online transaction processing, electronic data interchange (EDI), inventory management systems, and automated data collection systems.

a. Online shopping
b. A Stake in the Outcome
c. A4e
d. Electronic Commerce

Chapter 2. Strategic Management and the Entrepreneur

13. _____ or _____ data refers to selected population characteristics as used in government, marketing or opinion research, or the _____ profiles used in such research. Note the distinction from the term 'demography' Commonly-used _____s include race, age, income, disabilities, mobility (in terms of travel time to work or number of vehicles available), educational attainment, home ownership, employment status, and even location.
   a. Abraham Harold Maslow
   b. Demographic
   c. Adam Smith
   d. Affiliation

14. _____ is a worldwide management consulting firm that focuses on solving issues of concern to senior management. McKinsey serves as an advisor to the world's leading businesses, governments, and institutions. It is widely recognized as a leader and one of the most prestigious firms in the management consulting industry.
   a. 1990 Clean Air Act
   b. McKinsey ' Company
   c. 28-hour day
   d. 33 Strategies of War

15. _____ in marketing and strategic management is an assessment of the strengths and weaknesses of current and potential competitors. This analysis provides both an offensive and defensive strategic context through which to identify opportunities and threats. Competitor profiling coalesces all of the relevant sources of _____ into one framework in the support of efficient and effective strategy formulation, implementation, monitoring and adjustment.
   a. Competitor analysis
   b. Competitor or Competitive Intelligence
   c. 1990 Clean Air Act
   d. 28-hour day

16. A _____ is a relatively new executive level position at a corporation, company, organization typically reporting directly to the CEO or board of directors. The _____ is responsible for a brand's image, experience, and promise, and propagating it throughout all aspects of the company. The brand officer oversees marketing, advertising, design, public relations and customer service departments.
   a. Chief executive officer
   b. Director of communications
   c. Chief brand officer
   d. Purchasing manager

17. _____ is the process of comparing the cost, cycle time, productivity, or quality of a specific process or method to another that is widely considered to be an industry standard or best practice. Essentially, _____ provides a snapshot of the performance of your business and helps you understand where you are in relation to a particular standard. The result is often a business case for making changes in order to make improvements.
   a. Benchmarking
   b. Competitive heterogeneity
   c. Cost leadership
   d. Complementors

18. _____ is a contract between two parties, one being the employer and the other being the employee. An employee may be defined as: 'A person in the service of another under any contract of hire, express or implied, oral or written, where the employer has the power or right to control and direct the employee in the material details of how the work is to be performed.' Black's Law Dictionary page 471 (5th ed. 1979.)
   a. Exit interview
   b. Employment
   c. Employment counsellor
   d. Employment rate

19. A _____ is a set of exclusive rights granted by a state to an inventor or his assignee for a limited period of time in exchange for a disclosure of an invention.

Chapter 2. Strategic Management and the Entrepreneur

The procedure for granting _____s, the requirements placed on the _____ee and the extent of the exclusive rights vary widely between countries according to national laws and international agreements. Typically, however, a _____ application must include one or more claims defining the invention which must be new, inventive, and useful or industrially applicable.

a. Patent
b. Labor Management Reporting and Disclosure Act
c. Food, Drug, and Cosmetic Act
d. Federal Trade Commission Act

20. The U.S. _____ is an independent agency of the United States government which holds primary responsibility for enforcing the federal securities laws and regulating the securities industry, the nation's stock and options exchanges, and other electronic securities markets. The SEC was created by section 4 of the Securities Exchange Act of 1934 (now codified as 15 U.S.C. § 78d and commonly referred to as the 1934 Act.)

a. 1990 Clean Air Act
b. 28-hour day
c. 33 Strategies of War
d. Securities and Exchange Commission

21. _____ is an advertisement in which a particular product specifically mentions a competitor by name for the express purpose of showing why the competitor is inferior to the product naming it.

This should not be confused with parody advertisements, where a fictional product is being advertised for the purpose of poking fun at the particular advertisement, nor should it be confused with the use of a coined brand name for the purpose of comparing the product without actually naming an actual competitor. ('Wikipedia tastes better and is less filling than the Encyclopedia Galactica.')

In the 1980s, during what has been referred to as the cola wars, soft-drink manufacturer Pepsi ran a series of advertisements where people, caught on hidden camera, in a blind taste test, chose Pepsi over rival Coca-Cola.

a. Comparative advertising
b. 1990 Clean Air Act
c. 28-hour day
d. 33 Strategies of War

22. _____ systems are rule-based systems that are able to automatically provide solutions to repetitive management problems (Turban, Leidner, McLean and Wetherbe, 2007.) _____s are very closely related to business informatics and business analytics.

_____ systems are based on business rules.

a. Entertainment Management
b. Efficient Consumer Response
c. Executive development
d. Automated decision support

23. In finance, an _____ is a contract between a buyer and a seller that gives the buyer the right--but not the obligation--to buy or to sell a particular asset (the underlying asset) at a later day at an agreed price. In return for granting the _____, the seller collects a payment (the premium) from the buyer. A call _____ gives the buyer the right to buy the underlying asset; a put _____ gives the buyer of the _____ the right to sell the underlying asset.

a. AAAI
b. A Stake in the Outcome
c. A4e
d. Option

Chapter 2. Strategic Management and the Entrepreneur

24. In economics, business, retail, and accounting, a _____ is the value of money that has been used up to produce something, and hence is not available for use anymore. In economics, a _____ is an alternative that is given up as a result of a decision. In business, the _____ may be one of acquisition, in which case the amount of money expended to acquire it is counted as _____.

   a. Fixed costs
   b. Cost allocation
   c. Cost overrun
   d. Cost

25. _____ is a concept developed by Michael Porter, used in business strategy. It describes a way to establish the competitive advantage. _____, in basic words, means the lowest cost of operation in the industry.

   a. Switching cost
   b. Strategic group
   c. Strategic business unit
   d. Cost leadership

26. _____ has been described as the 'process of social influence in which one person can enlist the aid and support of others in the accomplishment of a common task'. A definition more inclusive of followers comes from Alan Keith of Genentech who said '_____ is ultimately about creating a way for people to contribute to making something extraordinary happen.'

   _____ is one of the most salient aspects of the organizational context. However, defining _____ has been challenging.

   a. Leadership
   b. 28-hour day
   c. Situational leadership
   d. 1990 Clean Air Act

27. _____, net margin, net _____ or net profit ratio all refer to a measure of profitability. It is calculated by finding the net profit as a percentage of the revenue.

$$\text{Net profit margin} = \frac{\text{Net profit (after taxes)}}{\text{Revenue}} \times 100\%$$

The _____ is mostly used for internal comparison.

   a. 1990 Clean Air Act
   b. Profit maximization
   c. Net profit margin
   d. Profit margin

28. The term '_____' refers to the concept of collecting information and attempting to spot a pattern in the information. In some fields of study, the term '_____' has more formally-defined meanings.

   In project management _____ is a mathematical technique that uses historical results to predict future outcome.

   a. Regression analysis
   b. Stepwise regression
   c. Least squares
   d. Trend analysis

29. _____ is one of the four Ps of the marketing mix. The other three aspects are product, promotion, and place. It is also a key variable in microeconomic price allocation theory.

Chapter 2. Strategic Management and the Entrepreneur

a. Pricing
c. Price floor
b. Penetration pricing
d. Transfer pricing

30. _____ is an integrated communications-based process through which individuals and communities discover that existing and newly-identified needs and wants may be satisfied by the products and services of others.

_____ is defined by the American _____ Association as the activity, set of institutions, and processes for creating, communicating, delivering, and exchanging offerings that have value for customers, clients, partners, and society at large. The term developed from the original meaning which referred literally to going to market, as in shopping, or going to a market to buy or sell goods or services.

a. Disruptive technology
c. Customer relationship management
b. Marketing
d. Market development

31. The _____ is a performance management tool for measuring whether the smaller-scale operational activities of a company are aligned with its larger-scale objectives in terms of vision and strategy.

By focusing not only on financial outcomes but also on the operational, marketing and developmental inputs to these, the _____ helps provide a more comprehensive view of a business, which in turn helps organizations act in their best long-term interests. This tool is also being used to address business response to climate change and greenhouse gas emissions.

a. Balanced scorecard
c. Middle management
b. Management development
d. Commercial management

32. _____ is one of the managerial functions like planning, organizing, staffing and directing. It is an important function because it helps to check the errors and to take the corrective action so that deviation from standards are minimized and stated goals of the organization are achieved in desired manner. According to modern concepts, _____ is a foreseeing action whereas earlier concept of _____ was used only when errors were detected. _____ in management means setting standards, measuring actual performance and taking corrective action.

a. Turnover
c. Schedule of reinforcement
b. Decision tree pruning
d. Control

33. _____ is a form of corporate self-regulation integrated into a business model. Ideally, _____ policy would function as a built-in, self-regulating mechanism whereby business would monitor and ensure their adherence to law, ethical standards, and international norms. Business would embrace responsibility for the impact of their activities on the environment, consumers, employees, communities, stakeholders and all other members of the public sphere.

a. 28-hour day
c. 1990 Clean Air Act
b. 33 Strategies of War
d. Corporate social responsibility

Chapter 3. Choosing a Form of Ownership 13

1. _____ was a writer, management consultant, and self-described 'social ecologist.' Widely considered to be 'the father of modern management,' his 39 books and countless scholarly and popular articles explored how humans are organized across all sectors of society--in business, government and the nonprofit world. His writings have predicted many of the major developments of the late twentieth century, including privatization and decentralization; the rise of Japan to economic world power; the decisive importance of marketing; and the emergence of the information society with its necessity of lifelong learning. In 1959, Drucker coined the term 'knowledge worker' and later in his life considered knowledge work productivity to be the next frontier of management.
   - a. Debora L. Spar
   - b. Peter Ferdinand Drucker
   - c. Chrissie Hynde
   - d. Jacques Al-Salawat Nasruddin Nasser

2. _____ is one of the managerial functions like planning, organizing, staffing and directing. It is an important function because it helps to check the errors and to take the corrective action so that deviation from standards are minimized and stated goals of the organization are achieved in desired manner. According to modern concepts, _____ is a foreseeing action whereas earlier concept of _____ was used only when errors were detected. _____ in management means setting standards, measuring actual performance and taking corrective action.
   - a. Control
   - b. Turnover
   - c. Schedule of reinforcement
   - d. Decision tree pruning

3. In economics, business, retail, and accounting, a _____ is the value of money that has been used up to produce something, and hence is not available for use anymore. In economics, a _____ is an alternative that is given up as a result of a decision. In business, the _____ may be one of acquisition, in which case the amount of money expended to acquire it is counted as _____.
   - a. Cost allocation
   - b. Cost
   - c. Cost overrun
   - d. Fixed costs

4. _____ according to Onuoha (2007) is the practice of starting new organizations or revitalizing mature organizations, particularly new businesses generally in response to identified opportunities. _____ is often a difficult undertaking, as a vast majority of new businesses fail. Entrepreneurial activities are substantially different depending on the type of organization that is being started.
   - a. A4e
   - b. AAAI
   - c. A Stake in the Outcome
   - d. Entrepreneurship

5. _____ is a concept whereby a person's financial liability is limited to a fixed sum, most commonly the value of a person's investment in a company or partnership with _____. In other words, if a company with _____ is sued, then the plaintiffs are suing the company, not its owners or investors. A shareholder in a limited company is not personally liable for any of the debts of the company, other than for the value of his investment in that company.
   - a. Limited liability
   - b. Toxic Substances Control Act
   - c. Partnership
   - d. Privity

6. _____ is the state or fact of exclusive rights and control over property, which may be an object, land/real estate or intellectual property. An _____ right is also referred to as title. The concept of _____ has existed for thousands of years and in all cultures.
   - a. A4e
   - b. Ownership
   - c. Emanation of the state
   - d. A Stake in the Outcome

Chapter 3. Choosing a Form of Ownership

7. _____ is a form of communication that typically attempts to persuade potential customers to purchase or to consume more of a particular brand of product or service. 'While now central to the contemporary global economy and the reproduction of global production networks, it is only quite recently that _____ has been more than a marginal influence on patterns of sales and production. The formation of modern _____ was intimately bound up with the emergence of new forms of monopoly capitalism around the end of the 19th and beginning of the 20th century as one element in corporate strategies to create, organize and where possible control markets, especially for mass produced consumer goods.
    a. AAAI
    b. A4e
    c. Advertising
    d. A Stake in the Outcome

8. A _____ is a formal statement of a set of business goals, the reasons why they are believed attainable, and the plan for reaching those goals. It may also contain background information about the organization or team attempting to reach those goals.

   The business goals may be defined for for-profit or for non-profit organizations.

    a. Time management
    b. Crisis management
    c. Distributed management
    d. Business plan

9. The _____ is a bank regulation, which sets a framework on how banks and depository institutions must handle their capital. The categorization of assets and capital is highly standardized so that it can be risk weighted. Internationally, the Basel Committee on Banking Supervision housed at the Bank for International Settlements influence each country's banking _____s.
    a. Capital requirement
    b. 1990 Clean Air Act
    c. Lock box
    d. Reserve requirement

10. A _____ is a corporation in the United States that, for Federal income tax purposes, is taxed under 26 U.S.C. § 11 and Subchapter C (26 U.S.C.
    a. 33 Strategies of War
    b. C corporation
    c. 1990 Clean Air Act
    d. 28-hour day

11. _____ is equal to the income that a firm has after subtracting costs and expenses from the total revenue. _____ can be distributed among holders of common stock as a dividend or held by the firm as retained earnings. _____ is an accounting term.
    a. Generally accepted accounting principles
    b. Net profit
    c. Matching principle
    d. Net income

12. A _____ is a type of business entity in which partners (owners) share with each other the profits or losses of the business. _____s are often favored over corporations for taxation purposes, as the _____ structure does not generally incur a tax on profits before it is distributed to the partners (i.e. there is no dividend tax levied.) However, depending on the _____ structure and the jurisdiction in which it operates, owners of a _____ may be exposed to greater personal liability than they would as shareholders of a corporation.
    a. Due process
    b. Mediation
    c. Partnership
    d. Federal Employers Liability Act

13. An _____, for United States federal income tax purposes, is a corporation that makes a valid election to be taxed under Subchapter S of Chapter 1 of the Internal Revenue Code.

Chapter 3. Choosing a Form of Ownership

In general, _____s do not pay any income taxes. Instead, the corporation's income or losses are divided among and passed through to its shareholders.

a. 28-hour day
c. 33 Strategies of War
b. 1990 Clean Air Act
d. S corporation

14. A _____ also known as a sole trader, or simply proprietorship is a type of business entity which there is only one owner and he has the final word taking all desicions by himself. All debts of the business are debts of the owner and must pay from his personal possessions. This means that the owner has unlimited liabilty.

a. Sole proprietorship
c. Golden hello
b. Business rule
d. Foreign ownership

15. _____ can be regarded as an outcome of mental processes (cognitive process) leading to the selection of a course of action among several alternatives. Every _____ process produces a final choice. The output can be an action or an opinion of choice.

a. 1990 Clean Air Act
c. 33 Strategies of War
b. 28-hour day
d. Decision making

16. _____ is an advertisement in which a particular product specifically mentions a competitor by name for the express purpose of showing why the competitor is inferior to the product naming it.

This should not be confused with parody advertisements, where a fictional product is being advertised for the purpose of poking fun at the particular advertisement, nor should it be confused with the use of a coined brand name for the purpose of comparing the product without actually naming an actual competitor. ('Wikipedia tastes better and is less filling than the Encyclopedia Galactica.')

In the 1980s, during what has been referred to as the cola wars, soft-drink manufacturer Pepsi ran a series of advertisements where people, caught on hidden camera, in a blind taste test, chose Pepsi over rival Coca-Cola.

a. 1990 Clean Air Act
c. 33 Strategies of War
b. 28-hour day
d. Comparative advertising

17. Articles of Partnership is a voluntary contract between two or among more than two persons to place their capital, labor, and skills, and corporation in business with the understanding that there will be a sharing of the profits and losses between/among partners. Outside of North America, it is normally referred to simply as a _____.

There are also multiple sections which are often included as well in articles of partnership, based on the circumstance.

a. Partnership agreement
c. Reverification
b. Foreign Corrupt Practices Act
d. Joint venture

Chapter 3. Choosing a Form of Ownership

18. In the commercial and legal parlance of most countries, a _____ or simply a partnership, refers to an association of persons or an unincorporated company with the following major features:

- Created by agreement, proof of existence and estoppel.
- Formed by two or more persons
- The owners are all personally liable for any legal actions and debts the company may face

It is a partnership in which partners share equally in both responsibility and liability.

Partnerships have certain default characteristics relating to both the relationship between the individual partners and (b) the relationship between the partnership and the outside world. The former can generally be overridden by agreement between the partners, whereas the latter generally cannot be.

The assets of the business are owned on behalf of the other partners, and they are each personally liable, jointly and severally, for business debts, taxes or tortious liability.

a. Business Roundtable
b. Prospero Business Suite
c. General partnership
d. National Center for Trauma-Informed Care

19. _____, also referred to simply as a 'public offering' or 'flotation,' is when a company issues common stock or shares to the public for the first time. They are often issued by smaller, younger companies seeking capital to expand, but can also be done by large privately-owned companies looking to become publicly traded.

In an _____ the issuer may obtain the assistance of an underwriting firm, which helps it determine what type of security to issue (common or preferred), best offering price and time to bring it to market.

a. Unemployment insurance
b. Occupational Safety and Health Administration
c. Outsourcing
d. Initial public offering

20. A _____ is a form of partnership similar to a general partnership, except that in addition to one or more general partners (GPs), there are one or more limited partners (_____s.) It is a partnership in which only one partner is required to be a general partner.

The GPs are, in all major respects, in the same legal position as partners in a conventional firm, i.e. they have management control, share the right to use partnership property, share the profits of the firm in predefined proportions, and have joint and several liability for the debts of the partnership.

a. Private equity
b. Growth capital
c. Pension fund
d. Limited partnership

21. A _____ is a business that is privately owned and operated, with a small number of employees and relatively low volume of sales. The legal definition of 'small' often varies by country and industry, but is generally under 100 employees in the United States and under 50 employees in the European Union. In comparison, the definition of mid-sized business by the number of employees is generally under 500 in the U.S. and 250 for the European Union.

Chapter 3. Choosing a Form of Ownership

a. Critical Success Factor
b. Pre-determined overhead rate
c. Golden Boot Compensation
d. Small Business

22. The _____ is a United States government agency that provides support to small businesses.

The mission of the _____ is 'to maintain and strengthen the nation's economy by enabling the establishment and viability of small businesses and by assisting in the economic recovery of communities after disasters.'

The _____ makes loans directly to businesses and acts as a guarantor on bank loans. In some circumstances it also makes loans to victims of natural disasters, works to get government procurement contracts for small businesses, and assists businesses with management, technical and training issues.

a. 28-hour day
b. 1990 Clean Air Act
c. Small Business Administration
d. 33 Strategies of War

23. A _____ is a relatively new executive level position at a corporation, company, organization typically reporting directly to the CEO or board of directors. The _____ is responsible for a brand's image, experience, and promise, and propagating it throughout all aspects of the company. The brand officer oversees marketing, advertising, design, public relations and customer service departments.

a. Purchasing manager
b. Chief executive officer
c. Director of communications
d. Chief brand officer

24. In the United Kingdom _____s are governed by the _____s Act 2000 (in England and Wales and Scotland) and the _____s Act (Northern Ireland) 2002 in Northern Ireland. A UK _____ is a Corporate body - that is to say, it has a continuing legal existence independent of its Members, as compared to a Partnership which may (in England and Wales they do not) have a legal existence dependent upon its Membership.

A UK _____'s members have a collective ('Joint') responsibility, to the extent that they may agree in an '_____ agreement', but no individual ('several') responsibility for each other's actions.

a. Compensation methods
b. Limited liability partnership
c. Chief risk officer
d. Small and medium enterprises

25. _____ can refer to a law of local or limited application, passed under the authority of a higher law specifying what things may be regulated by the _____, or it can refer to the internal rules of a company or organisation.

Corporate and organizational _____s regulate only the organisation to which they apply and are generally concerned with the operation of the organisation, setting out the form, manner or procedure in which a company or organisation should be run. Corporate _____s are drafted by a corporation's founders or directors under the authority of its Charter or Articles of Incorporation.

a. Racketeer Influenced and Corrupt Organizations Act
b. Fiduciary
c. Genuine Occupational Qualification
d. Bylaw

Chapter 3. Choosing a Form of Ownership

26. A _____ is a legal document relating to the formation of a company or corporation. It is a license to form a corporation issued by state government. Its precise meaning depends upon the legal system in which it is used, but the two primary meanings are:

- In the U.S.A. a _____ is usually used as an alternative description of a corporation's articles of incorporation.
- In English and Commonwealth legal systems, a _____ is usually a simple certificate issued by the relevant government registry as confirmation of the due incorporation and valid existence of the company.

In the U.S.A. the _____ or articles of incorporation form a major constituent part of the constitutional documents of the corporation.

a. Blue sky law
c. Toxic Substances Control Act
b. Certificate of Incorporation
d. Civil Rights Act of 1875

27. _____ is a contractual right that gives its holder the option to enter a business transaction with the owner of something, according to specified terms, before the owner is entitled to enter into that transaction with a third party. In brief, the _____ is similar in concept to a call option.

An _____ can cover almost any sort of asset, including real estate, personal property, a patent license, a screenplay, or an interest in a business.

a. 33 Strategies of War
c. 1990 Clean Air Act
b. Right of first refusal
d. 28-hour day

28. A mutual shareholder or _____ is an individual or company (including a corporation) that legally owns one or more shares of stock in a joint stock company. A company's shareholders collectively own that company. Thus, the typical goal of such companies is to enhance shareholder value.

a. 1990 Clean Air Act
c. Shareholder
b. Stockholder
d. Free riding

29. A _____ or reacquired stock is stock which is bought back by the issuing company, reducing the amount of outstanding stock on the open market ('open market' including insiders' holdings.)

Stock repurchases are often used as a tax-efficient method to put cash into shareholders' hands, rather than pay dividends. Sometimes, companies do this when they feel that their stock is undervalued on the open market.

a. Generally accepted accounting principles
c. Current liabilities
b. Treasury stock
d. Matching principle

30. A _____ is a funding round of securities which are sold without a initial public offering, usually to a small number of chosen private investors. In the United States, these placements are not subject to the Securities Act of 1933 and do not have to be registered with the Securities and Exchange Commission, although the sale must conform to SEC rules. _____s may typically consist of stocks, shares or warrants and purchasers are often institutional investors such as banks, insurance companies or pension funds.

a. Choquet integral
b. Labor intensive
c. Niche market
d. Private placement

31. _____ is the imposition of two or more taxes on the same income (in the case of income taxes), asset (in the case of capital taxes), or financial transaction (in the case of sales taxes.) It refers to two distinct situations:

- taxation of dividend income without relief or credit for taxes paid by the company paying the dividend on the income from which the dividend is paid. This arises in the so-called 'classical' system of corporate taxation, used in the United States.
- taxation by two or more countries of the same income, asset or transaction, for example income paid by an entity of one country to a resident of a different country. The double liability is often mitigated by tax treaties between countries.

It is not unusual for a business or individual who is resident in one country to make a taxable gain (earnings, profits) in another. This person may find that he is obliged by domestic laws to pay tax on that gain locally and pay again in the country in which the gain was made. Since this is inequitable, many nations make bilateral _____ agreements with each other.

a. Tax evasion
b. Federal Unemployment Tax Act
c. Double taxation
d. Federal Reserve Banks

32. The U.S. _____ is an independent agency of the United States government which holds primary responsibility for enforcing the federal securities laws and regulating the securities industry, the nation's stock and options exchanges, and other electronic securities markets. The SEC was created by section 4 of the Securities Exchange Act of 1934 (now codified as 15 U.S.C. § 78d and commonly referred to as the 1934 Act.)

a. 1990 Clean Air Act
b. 33 Strategies of War
c. Securities and Exchange Commission
d. 28-hour day

33. In economics and sociology, an _____ is any factor (financial or non-financial) that enables or motivates a particular course of action, or counts as a reason for preferring one choice to the alternatives. It is an expectation that encourages people to behave in a certain way. Since human beings are purposeful creatures, the study of _____ structures is central to the study of all economic activity (both in terms of individual decision-making and in terms of co-operation and competition within a larger institutional structure.)

a. AAAI
b. A Stake in the Outcome
c. A4e
d. Incentive

34. A _____ in the law of the vast majority of United States jurisdictions is a legal form of business company that provides limited liability to its owners. Often incorrectly called a 'limited liability corporation' (instead of company), it is a hybrid business entity having certain characteristics of both a corporation and a partnership or sole proprietorship (depending on how many owners there are.) The primary characteristic an _____ shares with a corporation is limited liability, and the primary characteristic it shares with a partnership is the availability of pass-through income taxation.

a. Venture Capitalist
b. Growth capital
c. Limited liability company
d. Limited partners

Chapter 3. Choosing a Form of Ownership

35. A _____ is an entity formed between two or more parties to undertake economic activity together. The parties agree to create a new entity by both contributing equity, and they then share in the revenues, expenses, and control of the enterprise. The venture can be for one specific project only, or a continuing business relationship such as the Fuji Xerox _____.
   a. Joint venture
   b. Civil Rights Act of 1991
   c. Patent
   d. Meritor Savings Bank v. Vinson

36. An _____ is a person who has possession of an enterprise and assumes significant accountability for the inherent risks and the outcome. It is an ambitious leader who combines land, labor, and capital to create and market new goods or services. The term is a loanword from French and was first defined by the Irish economist Richard Cantillon.
   a. A4e
   b. A Stake in the Outcome
   c. AAAI
   d. Entrepreneur

37. Market _____ is a business, economics or investment term that refers to an asset's ability to be easily converted through an act of buying or selling without causing a significant movement in the price and with minimum loss of value. Money, or cash on hand, is the most liquid asset. An act of exchange of a less liquid asset with a more liquid asset is called liquidation.
   a. 28-hour day
   b. 33 Strategies of War
   c. 1990 Clean Air Act
   d. Liquidity

Chapter 4. Franchising and the Entrepreneur

1. _____ refers to the methods of practicing and using another person's business philosophy. The franchisor grants the independent operator the right to distribute its products, techniques, and trademarks for a percentage of gross monthly sales and a royalty fee. Various tangibles and intangibles such as national or international advertising, training, and other support services are commonly made available by the franchisor.

   a. ServiceMaster
   b. Franchising
   c. 28-hour day
   d. 1990 Clean Air Act

2. The _____ is an independent agency of the United States government, established in 1914 by the _____ Act. Its principal mission is the promotion of 'consumer protection' and the elimination and prevention of what regulators perceive to be harmfully 'anti-competitive' business practices, such as coercive monopoly.

   The _____ Act was one of President Wilson's major acts against trusts.

   a. 28-hour day
   b. Federal Trade Commission
   c. 33 Strategies of War
   d. 1990 Clean Air Act

3. Franchising refers to the methods of practicing and using another person's business philosophy. The _____ grants the independent operator the right to distribute its products, techniques, and trademarks for a percentage of gross monthly sales and a royalty fee. Various tangibles and intangibles such as national or international advertising, training, and other support services are commonly made available by the _____.

   a. Franchisor
   b. 28-hour day
   c. ServiceMaster
   d. 1990 Clean Air Act

4. _____ is an abbreviation for '_____', a legal document used in the franchising process in the United States.

   Franchisors must give a _____ to franchisees at least 10 business days before any contract is signed and before any money changes hands. It contains extensive information about a franchisor, which is intended to give potential franchisees enough information to make educated decisions about their investments.

   a. A4e
   b. AAAI
   c. A Stake in the Outcome
   d. Uniform Franchise Offering Circular

5. _____ is one of the four elements of marketing mix. An organization or set of organizations (go-betweens) involved in the process of making a product or service available for use or consumption by a consumer or business user.

   The other three parts of the marketing mix are product, pricing, and promotion.

   a. Matching theory
   b. Job creation programs
   c. Missing completely at random
   d. Distribution

6. _____ is a form of communication that typically attempts to persuade potential customers to purchase or to consume more of a particular brand of product or service. 'While now central to the contemporary global economy and the reproduction of global production networks, it is only quite recently that _____ has been more than a marginal influence on patterns of sales and production. The formation of modern _____ was intimately bound up with the emergence of new forms of monopoly capitalism around the end of the 19th and beginning of the 20th century as one element in corporate strategies to create, organize and where possible control markets, especially for mass produced consumer goods.

a. A4e
c. AAAI
b. A Stake in the Outcome
d. Advertising

7. A _____ is a name or trademark connected with a product or producer. _____s have become increasingly important components of culture and the economy, now being described as 'cultural accessories and personal philosophies'.

Some people distinguish the psychological aspect of a _____ from the experiential aspect.

a. Brand loyalty
c. Brand extension
b. Brand
d. Brand awareness

8. _____ is an advertisement in which a particular product specifically mentions a competitor by name for the express purpose of showing why the competitor is inferior to the product naming it.

This should not be confused with parody advertisements, where a fictional product is being advertised for the purpose of poking fun at the particular advertisement, nor should it be confused with the use of a coined brand name for the purpose of comparing the product without actually naming an actual competitor. ('Wikipedia tastes better and is less filling than the Encyclopedia Galactica.')

In the 1980s, during what has been referred to as the cola wars, soft-drink manufacturer Pepsi ran a series of advertisements where people, caught on hidden camera, in a blind taste test, chose Pepsi over rival Coca-Cola.

a. Comparative advertising
c. 1990 Clean Air Act
b. 33 Strategies of War
d. 28-hour day

9. A _____ is a business that is privately owned and operated, with a small number of employees and relatively low volume of sales. The legal definition of 'small' often varies by country and industry, but is generally under 100 employees in the United States and under 50 employees in the European Union. In comparison, the definition of mid-sized business by the number of employees is generally under 500 in the U.S. and 250 for the European Union.

a. Small Business
c. Critical Success Factor
b. Pre-determined overhead rate
d. Golden Boot Compensation

10. The _____ is a United States government agency that provides support to small businesses.

The mission of the _____ is 'to maintain and strengthen the nation's economy by enabling the establishment and viability of small businesses and by assisting in the economic recovery of communities after disasters.'

The _____ makes loans directly to businesses and acts as a guarantor on bank loans. In some circumstances it also makes loans to victims of natural disasters, works to get government procurement contracts for small businesses, and assists businesses with management, technical and training issues.

a. 28-hour day
c. 33 Strategies of War
b. 1990 Clean Air Act
d. Small Business Administration

11. The _____ is the Cabinet department of the United States government concerned with promoting economic growth. It was originally created as the _____ and Labor on February 14, 1903. It was subsequently renamed to the Department of Commerce on March 4, 1913, and its bureaus and agencies specializing in labor were transferred to the new Department of Labor.
   a. A4e
   b. AAAI
   c. A Stake in the Outcome
   d. United States Department of Commerce

12. In economics, business, retail, and accounting, a _____ is the value of money that has been used up to produce something, and hence is not available for use anymore. In economics, a _____ is an alternative that is given up as a result of a decision. In business, the _____ may be one of acquisition, in which case the amount of money expended to acquire it is counted as _____.
   a. Cost overrun
   b. Fixed costs
   c. Cost allocation
   d. Cost

13. There are many important decisions about product and service development and marketing. In the process of product development and marketing we should focus on strategic decisions about product attributes, product branding, product packaging, product labeling and product support services. But product strategy also calls for building a _____.
   a. Context analysis
   b. Product line
   c. Marketing strategy
   d. Product bundling

14.

The _____ can vary from one organization to another but there are some key elements that are common throughout

The process usually starts with a 'Demand' or requirements - this could be for a physical part (inventory) or a service. A requisition is generated, which details the requirements (in some cases providing a requirements speciation) which actions the procurement department. An RFP or RFQ is then raised (request for proposal or Request for quotation.)

   a. Request for quotation
   b. Purchase requisition
   c. 1990 Clean Air Act
   d. Purchasing process

15. _____ is a term used for a number of concepts involving either the performance of an investigation of a business or person, or the performance of an act with a certain standard of care. It can be a legal obligation, but the term will more commonly apply to voluntary investigations. A common example of _____ in various industries is the process through which a potential acquirer evaluates a target company or its assets for acquisition.
   a. Technology transfer
   b. Negligence in employment
   c. Flextime
   d. Due diligence

16. Marketing research is a form of business research and is generally divided into two categories: consumer _____ and business-to-business (B2B) _____, which was previously known as industrial marketing research. Consumer marketing research studies the buying habits of individual people while business-to-business marketing research investigates the markets for products sold by one business to another.

Chapter 4. Franchising and the Entrepreneur

Consumer _____ is a form of applied sociology that concentrates on understanding the behaviours, whims and preferences, of consumers in a market-based economy, and aims to understand the effects and comparative success of marketing campaigns.

a. Questionnaire
b. Mystery shoppers
c. Questionnaire construction
d. Market research

17. An _____ is a person who has possession of an enterprise and assumes significant accountability for the inherent risks and the outcome. It is an ambitious leader who combines land, labor, and capital to create and market new goods or services. The term is a loanword from French and was first defined by the Irish economist Richard Cantillon.

a. Entrepreneur
b. A Stake in the Outcome
c. AAAI
d. A4e

18. _____ is an integrated communications-based process through which individuals and communities discover that existing and newly-identified needs and wants may be satisfied by the products and services of others.

_____ is defined by the American _____ Association as the activity, set of institutions, and processes for creating, communicating, delivering, and exchanging offerings that have value for customers, clients, partners, and society at large. The term developed from the original meaning which referred literally to going to market, as in shopping, or going to a market to buy or sell goods or services.

a. Customer relationship management
b. Disruptive technology
c. Market development
d. Marketing

19. A _____ is a distinctive sign or indicator used by an individual, business organization, or other legal entity to identify that the products and/or services to consumers with which the _____ appears originate from a unique source and to distinguish its products or services from those of other entities.

a. Kanban
b. Virtual team
c. Trademark
d. Succession planning

20. In a human resources context, _____ or labor _____ is the rate at which an employer gains and loses employees. Simple ways to describe it are 'how long employees tend to stay' or 'the rate of traffic through the revolving door.' _____ is measured for individual companies and for their industry as a whole. If an employer is said to have a high _____ relative to its competitors, it means that employees of that company have a shorter average tenure than those of other companies in the same industry.

a. Ten year occupational employment projection
b. Continuous
c. Career portfolios
d. Turnover

21. _____ can be regarded as an outcome of mental processes (cognitive process) leading to the selection of a course of action among several alternatives. Every _____ process produces a final choice. The output can be an action or an opinion of choice.

a. 33 Strategies of War
b. 28-hour day
c. 1990 Clean Air Act
d. Decision making

Chapter 4. Franchising and the Entrepreneur

22. The term '_____' refers to the concept of collecting information and attempting to spot a pattern in the information. In some fields of study, the term '_____' has more formally-defined meanings.

In project management _____ is a mathematical technique that uses historical results to predict future outcome.

 a. Trend analysis
 b. Stepwise regression
 c. Least squares
 d. Regression analysis

23. _____, commonly known as e-commerce, consists of the buying and selling of products or services over electronic systems such as the Internet and other computer networks. The amount of trade conducted electronically has grown extraordinarily with widespread Internet usage. The use of commerce is conducted in this way, spurring and drawing on innovations in electronic funds transfer, supply chain management, Internet marketing, online transaction processing, electronic data interchange (EDI), inventory management systems, and automated data collection systems.

 a. A Stake in the Outcome
 b. A4e
 c. Online shopping
 d. Electronic Commerce

24. _____ refers to several different marketing arrangements:

_____ is when two companies form an alliance to work together, creating marketing synergy. As described in _____: The Science of Alliance:

_____ is an arrangement that associates a single product or service with more than one brand name, or otherwise associates a product with someone other than the principal producer. The typical _____ agreement involves two or more companies acting in cooperation to associate any of various logos, color schemes, or brand identifiers to a specific product that is contractually designated for this purpose.

 a. 1990 Clean Air Act
 b. 33 Strategies of War
 c. Co-branding
 d. 28-hour day

25. A _____ is a framework for creating economic, social, and/or other forms of value. The term _____ is thus used for a broad range of informal and formal descriptions to represent core aspects of a business, including purpose, offerings, strategies, infrastructure, organizational structures, trading practices, and operational processes and policies.

Conceptualizations of _____s try to formalize informal descriptions into building blocks and their relationships.

 a. Business model
 b. Gap analysis
 c. Business networking
 d. Business model design

26. _____ of the learning curve effect and the closely related experience curve effect express the relationship between equations for experience and efficiency or between efficiency gains and investment in the effort. The experience of 'learning curves' was first observed by the 19th Century German psychologist Hermann Ebbinghaus according to the difficulty of memorizing varying numbers of verbal stimuli, and subsequent learning about the complex processes of learning are discussed in the

The rule used for representing the learning curve effect states that the more times a task has been performed, the less time will be required on each subsequent iteration.

a. Point biserial correlation coefficient
b. Spatial Decision Support Systems
c. Models
d. Distribution

27. A _____ is a set of exclusive rights granted by a state to an inventor or his assignee for a limited period of time in exchange for a disclosure of an invention.

The procedure for granting _____s, the requirements placed on the _____ee and the extent of the exclusive rights vary widely between countries according to national laws and international agreements. Typically, however, a _____ application must include one or more claims defining the invention which must be new, inventive, and useful or industrially applicable.

a. Federal Trade Commission Act
b. Labor Management Reporting and Disclosure Act
c. Food, Drug, and Cosmetic Act
d. Patent

Chapter 5. Buying an Existing Business

1. The phrase mergers and _____s refers to the aspect of corporate strategy, corporate finance and management dealing with the buying, selling and combining of different companies that can aid, finance, or help a growing company in a given industry grow rapidly without having to create another business entity.

An _____, also known as a takeover or a buyout, is the buying of one company (the 'target') by another. An _____ may be friendly or hostile.

a. AAAI
b. A Stake in the Outcome
c. A4e
d. Acquisition

2. _____ refers to the movement of cash into or out of a business or financial product. It is usually measured during a specified, finite period of time. Measurement of _____ can be used

- to determine a project's rate of return or value. The time of _____s into and out of projects are used as inputs in financial models such as internal rate of return, and net present value.
- to determine problems with a business's liquidity. Being profitable does not necessarily mean being liquid. A company can fail because of a shortage of cash, even while profitable.
- as an alternate measure of a business's profits when it is believed that accrual accounting concepts do not represent economic realities. For example, a company may be notionally profitable but generating little operational cash (as may be the case for a company that barters its products rather than selling for cash.) In such a case, the company may be deriving additional operating cash by issuing shares evaluating default risk, re-investment requirements, etc.

_____ is a generic term used differently depending on the context. It may be defined by users for their own purposes.

a. Gross profit margin
b. Gross profit
c. Sweat equity
d. Cash flow

3. _____ is one of a series of accounting transactions dealing with the billing of customers who owe money to a person, company or organization for goods and services that have been provided to the customer. In most business entities this is typically done by generating an invoice and mailing or electronically delivering it to the customer, who in turn must pay it within an established timeframe called credit or payment terms.

An example of a common payment term is Net 30, meaning payment is due in the amount of the invoice 30 days from the date of invoice.

a. Accumulated Depreciation
b. Accounts receivable
c. A Stake in the Outcome
d. Other revenue

4. In business and accounting, _____s are everything of value that is owned by a person or company. Any property or object of value that one possesses, usually considered as applicable to the payment of one's debts is considered an _____. Simplistically stated, _____s are things of value that can be readily converted into cash.

a. Asset
b. A4e
c. A Stake in the Outcome
d. AAAI

Chapter 5. Buying an Existing Business

5. _____ exists when one firm provides goods or services to a customer with an agreement to bill them later, or receive a shipment or service from a supplier under an agreement to pay them later. It can be viewed as an essential element of capitalization in an operating business because it can reduce the required capital investment to operate the business if it is managed properly. _____ is the largest use of capital for a majority of business to business (B2B) sellers in the United States and is a critical source of capital for a majority of all businesses.
   a. Countertrade
   b. 1990 Clean Air Act
   c. Trade credit
   d. Buy-sell agreement

6. In financial accounting, a _____ or statement of financial position is a summary of a person's or organization's balances. Assets, liabilities and ownership equity are listed as of a specific date, such as the end of its financial year. A _____ is often described as a snapshot of a company's financial condition.
   a. 1990 Clean Air Act
   b. 28-hour day
   c. Balance sheet
   d. 33 Strategies of War

7. _____ is a broad label that refers to any individuals or households that use goods and services generated within the economy. The concept of a _____ is used in different contexts, so that the usage and significance of the term may vary.

   Typically when business people and economists talk of _____s they are talking about person as _____, an aggregated commodity item with little individuality other than that expressed in the buy/not-buy decision.

   a. 28-hour day
   b. Consumer
   c. 1990 Clean Air Act
   d. 33 Strategies of War

8. An _____ is a sum paid by A to B by way of compensation for a particular loss suffered by B. The indemnifying party (A) may or may not be responsible for the loss suffered by the indemnified party (B.) Forms of _____ include cash payments, repairs, replacement, and reinstatement.

   In common parlance, _____ is often used as a synonym for compensation or reparation.

   a. Indemnity
   b. AAAI
   c. A Stake in the Outcome
   d. A4e

9. _____ is a document outlining an agreement between two or more parties before the agreement is finalized. The concept is similar to the so-called heads of agreement. Such agreements may be Asset Purchase Agreements, Share Purchase Agreements, Joint-Venture Agreements and overall all Agreements which aim at closing a financially large deal.
   a. Letter of intent
   b. 1990 Clean Air Act
   c. 33 Strategies of War
   d. 28-hour day

10. A _____ is a business that is privately owned and operated, with a small number of employees and relatively low volume of sales. The legal definition of 'small' often varies by country and industry, but is generally under 100 employees in the United States and under 50 employees in the European Union. In comparison, the definition of mid-sized business by the number of employees is generally under 500 in the U.S. and 250 for the European Union.

Chapter 5. Buying an Existing Business

a. Critical Success Factor
c. Pre-determined overhead rate
b. Small Business
d. Golden Boot Compensation

11. The _____ is a United States government agency that provides support to small businesses.

The mission of the _____ is 'to maintain and strengthen the nation's economy by enabling the establishment and viability of small businesses and by assisting in the economic recovery of communities after disasters.'

The _____ makes loans directly to businesses and acts as a guarantor on bank loans. In some circumstances it also makes loans to victims of natural disasters, works to get government procurement contracts for small businesses, and assists businesses with management, technical and training issues.

a. 33 Strategies of War
c. 1990 Clean Air Act
b. 28-hour day
d. Small Business Administration

12. _____ is a term used for a number of concepts involving either the performance of an investigation of a business or person, or the performance of an act with a certain standard of care. It can be a legal obligation, but the term will more commonly apply to voluntary investigations. A common example of _____ in various industries is the process through which a potential acquirer evaluates a target company or its assets for acquisition.

a. Flextime
c. Due diligence
b. Technology transfer
d. Negligence in employment

13.

The _____ can vary from one organization to another but there are some key elements that are common throughout

The process usually starts with a 'Demand' or requirements - this could be for a physical part (inventory) or a service. A requisition is generated, which details the requirements (in some cases providing a requirements speciation) which actions the procurement department. An RFP or RFQ is then raised (request for proposal or Request for quotation.)

a. Request for quotation
c. 1990 Clean Air Act
b. Purchase requisition
d. Purchasing process

14. _____ is an integrated communications-based process through which individuals and communities discover that existing and newly-identified needs and wants may be satisfied by the products and services of others.

_____ is defined by the American _____ Association as the activity, set of institutions, and processes for creating, communicating, delivering, and exchanging offerings that have value for customers, clients, partners, and society at large. The term developed from the original meaning which referred literally to going to market, as in shopping, or going to a market to buy or sell goods or services.

a. Disruptive technology
b. Market development
c. Customer relationship management
d. Marketing

15. _____ are defined as identifiable non-monetary assets that cannot be seen, touched or physically measured, which are created through time and/or effort and that are identifiable as a separate asset. There are two primary forms of intangibles - legal intangibles (such as trade secrets (e.g., customer lists), copyrights, patents, trademarks, and goodwill) and competitive intangibles (such as knowledge activities (know-how, knowledge), collaboration activities, leverage activities, and structural activities.) Legal intangibles are known under the generic term intellectual property and generate legal property rights defensible in a court of law.
    a. Employee value proposition
    b. Interlocking directorate
    c. Induction programme
    d. Intangible assets

16. _____ in marketing and strategic management is an assessment of the strengths and weaknesses of current and potential competitors. This analysis provides both an offensive and defensive strategic context through which to identify opportunities and threats. Competitor profiling coalesces all of the relevant sources of _____ into one framework in the support of efficient and effective strategy formulation, implementation, monitoring and adjustment.
    a. 1990 Clean Air Act
    b. 28-hour day
    c. Competitor analysis
    d. Competitor or Competitive Intelligence

17. _____ is a process and a set of procedures used to estimate the economic value of an owner's interest in a business. Valuation is used by financial market participants to determine the price they are willing to pay or receive to consummate a sale of a business. In addition to estimating the selling price of a business, the same valuation tools are often used by business appraisers to resolve disputes related to estate and gift taxation, divorce litigation, allocate business purchase price among business assets, establish a formula for estimating the value of partners' ownership interest for buy-sell agreements, and many other business and legal purposes.
    a. Munn v. Illinois
    b. No-FEAR Act
    c. Robinson-Patman Act
    d. Business valuation

18. _____ is the activity that the selling organization undertakes to reduce customer account defections. The success of this activity is when the customer account places an additional order before a 12-month period has expired. Note that ideally these orders will need to contribute similar financial amounts to the previous 12 months.
    a. Process automation
    b. Foreign ownership
    c. Business rule
    d. Customer retention

19. The _____, first published in 1952, is one of a number of uniform acts that have been promulgated in conjunction with efforts to harmonize the law of sales and other commercial transactions in all 50 states within the United States of America. This objective is deemed important because of the prevalence of commercial transactions that extend beyond one state (for example, where the goods are manufactured in state A, warehoused in state B, sold from state C and delivered in state D.) The _____ deals primarily with transactions involving personal property (movable property), not real property (immovable property.)
    a. A4e
    b. AAAI
    c. A Stake in the Outcome
    d. Uniform Commercial Code

Chapter 5. Buying an Existing Business

20. Title _____s serve as guarantees to the recipient of property, ensuring that the recipient receives what he or she bargained for. The English _____s of title, sometimes included in deeds to real property, are that the grantor is lawfully seized (in fee simple) of the property, (2) that the grantor has the right to convey the property to the grantee, (3) that the property is conveyed without encumbrances (this _____ is frequently modified to allow for certain encumbrances), (4) that the grantor has done no act to encumber the property, (5) that the grantee shall have quiet possession of the property, and (6) that the grantor will execute such further assurances of the land as may be requisite (Nos. 3 and 4, which overlap significantly, are sometimes treated as one item.)

a. Business valuation
b. Covenant
c. Hostile work environment
d. Trade secret

21. _____ is the term used to refer to the standard framework of guidelines for financial accounting used in any given jurisdiction. _____ includes the standards, conventions, and rules accountants follow in recording and summarizing transactions, and in the preparation of financial statements.

Financial accounting is information that must be assembled and reported objectively.

a. Depreciation
b. Net income
c. Generally accepted accounting principles
d. Treasury stock

22. _____ is a company's financial statement that indicates how the revenue is transformed into the net income The purpose of the _____ is to show managers and investors whether the company made or lost money during the period being reported.

The important thing to remember about an _____ is that it represents a period of time.

a. Income statement
b. A4e
c. A Stake in the Outcome
d. AAAI

23. An _____ is a tax levied on the financial income of people, corporations, or other legal entities. Various _____ systems exist, with varying degrees of tax incidence. Income taxation can be progressive, proportional, or regressive.

a. Ordinary income
b. Income tax
c. A4e
d. A Stake in the Outcome

24. The field of _____ looks at the relationship between management and workers, particularly groups of workers represented by a union.

_____ is an important factor in analyzing 'varieties of capitalism', such as neocorporatism, social democracy, and neoliberalism

a. Organizational effectiveness
b. Industrial relations
c. Informal organization
d. Overtime

25. _____ is the area of law in which manufacturers, distributors, suppliers, retailers, and others who make products available to the public are held responsible for the injuries those products cause.

Chapter 5. Buying an Existing Business

In the United States, the claims most commonly associated with _____ are negligence, strict liability, breach of warranty, and various consumer protection claims. The majority of _____ laws are determined at the state level and vary widely from state to state.

a. Railway Labor Act
b. Leave of absence
c. Right-to-work laws
d. Product liability

26. _____ are formal records of the financial activities of a business, person, or other entity. In British English, including United Kingdom company law, _____ are often referred to as accounts, although the term _____ is also used, particularly by accountants.

_____ provide an overview of a business or person's financial condition in both short and long term.

a. 28-hour day
b. Financial statements
c. 33 Strategies of War
d. 1990 Clean Air Act

27. _____ or economic opportunity loss is the value of the next best alternative forgone as the result of making a decision. _____ analysis is an important part of a company's decision-making processes but is not treated as an actual cost in any financial statement. The next best thing that a person can engage in is referred to as the _____ of doing the best thing and ignoring the next best thing to be done.

a. A4e
b. A Stake in the Outcome
c. AAAI
d. Opportunity cost

28. In economics, business, retail, and accounting, a _____ is the value of money that has been used up to produce something, and hence is not available for use anymore. In economics, a _____ is an alternative that is given up as a result of a decision. In business, the _____ may be one of acquisition, in which case the amount of money expended to acquire it is counted as _____.

a. Cost allocation
b. Cost
c. Cost overrun
d. Fixed costs

29. In business, _____ is the total liabilities minus total outside assets of an individual or a company. For a company, this is called shareholders' preference and may be referred to as book value. _____ is stated as at a particular year in time.

a. Net worth
b. Payback period
c. Novated lease
d. Deferred compensation

30. _____ is the value on a given date of a future payment or series of future payments, discounted to reflect the time value of money and other factors such as investment risk. _____ calculations are widely used in business and economics to provide a means to compare cash flows at different times on a meaningful 'like to like' basis.

If offered a choice between $100 today or $100 in one year, everyone will choose $100 today.

a. Present value
b. Net present value
c. 1990 Clean Air Act
d. Discounted cash flow

Chapter 5. Buying an Existing Business

31. An _____ is any party that makes an investment.

The term has taken on a specific meaning in finance to describe the particular types of people and companies that regularly purchase equity or debt securities for financial gain in exchange for funding an expanding company. Less frequently, the term is applied to parties who purchase real estate, currency, commodity derivatives, personal property, or other assets.

   a. AAAI
   c. A Stake in the Outcome
   b. Investor
   d. A4e

32. _____ is the corporate management term for the act of reorganizing the legal, ownership, operational, or other structures of a company for the purpose of making it more profitable, or better organized for its present needs. Alternate reasons for _____ include a change of ownership or ownership structure, demerger repositioning debt _____ and financial _____.

   a. Market value
   c. Market value added
   b. Net worth
   d. Restructuring

33. A _____ is a type of business entity in which partners (owners) share with each other the profits or losses of the business. _____s are often favored over corporations for taxation purposes, as the _____ structure does not generally incur a tax on profits before it is distributed to the partners (i.e. there is no dividend tax levied.) However, depending on the _____ structure and the jurisdiction in which it operates, owners of a _____ may be exposed to greater personal liability than they would as shareholders of a corporation.

   a. Due process
   c. Mediation
   b. Federal Employers Liability Act
   d. Partnership

34. A _____ is a form of partnership similar to a general partnership, except that in addition to one or more general partners (GPs), there are one or more limited partners (_____s.) It is a partnership in which only one partner is required to be a general partner.

The GPs are, in all major respects, in the same legal position as partners in a conventional firm, i.e. they have management control, share the right to use partnership property, share the profits of the firm in predefined proportions, and have joint and several liability for the debts of the partnership.

   a. Private equity
   c. Limited partnership
   b. Growth capital
   d. Pension fund

35. _____ is the state or fact of exclusive rights and control over property, which may be an object, land/real estate or intellectual property. An _____ right is also referred to as title. The concept of _____ has existed for thousands of years and in all cultures.

   a. A4e
   c. Emanation of the state
   b. Ownership
   d. A Stake in the Outcome

Chapter 6. Conducting a Feasibility Analysis and Crafting a Winning Business Plan

1. A _____ is a formal statement of a set of business goals, the reasons why they are believed attainable, and the plan for reaching those goals. It may also contain background information about the organization or team attempting to reach those goals.

The business goals may be defined for for-profit or for non-profit organizations.

   a. Distributed management
   b. Business plan
   c. Crisis management
   d. Time management

2. _____ is a form of communication that typically attempts to persuade potential customers to purchase or to consume more of a particular brand of product or service. 'While now central to the contemporary global economy and the reproduction of global production networks, it is only quite recently that _____ has been more than a marginal influence on patterns of sales and production. The formation of modern _____ was intimately bound up with the emergence of new forms of monopoly capitalism around the end of the 19th and beginning of the 20th century as one element in corporate strategies to create, organize and where possible control markets, especially for mass produced consumer goods.
   a. A4e
   b. AAAI
   c. A Stake in the Outcome
   d. Advertising

3. _____ generally refers to a list of all planned expenses and revenues. It is a plan for saving and spending. A _____ is an important concept in microeconomics, which uses a _____ line to illustrate the trade-offs between two or more goods.
   a. 28-hour day
   b. 1990 Clean Air Act
   c. 33 Strategies of War
   d. Budget

4. _____ is a concept related to the relative abilities of parties in a situation to exert influence over each other. If both parties are on an equal footing in a debate, then they will have equal _____, such as in a perfectly competitive market, or between an evenly matched monopoly and monopsony.

There are a number of fields where the concept of _____ has proven crucial to coherent analysis: game theory, labour economics, collective bargaining arrangements, diplomatic negotiations, settlement of litigation, the price of insurance, and any negotiation in general.

   a. Buy-sell agreement
   b. Trade credit
   c. Bargaining power
   d. 1990 Clean Air Act

5. _____ is an advertisement in which a particular product specifically mentions a competitor by name for the express purpose of showing why the competitor is inferior to the product naming it.

This should not be confused with parody advertisements, where a fictional product is being advertised for the purpose of poking fun at the particular advertisement, nor should it be confused with the use of a coined brand name for the purpose of comparing the product without actually naming an actual competitor. ('Wikipedia tastes better and is less filling than the Encyclopedia Galactica.')

In the 1980s, during what has been referred to as the cola wars, soft-drink manufacturer Pepsi ran a series of advertisements where people, caught on hidden camera, in a blind taste test, chose Pepsi over rival Coca-Cola.

Chapter 6. Conducting a Feasibility Analysis and Crafting a Winning Business Plan   35

a. 28-hour day
b. 1990 Clean Air Act
c. 33 Strategies of War
d. Comparative advertising

6. _____ is an unconventional system of promotions that relies on time, energy and imagination rather than a big marketing budget. Typically, _____ tactics are unexpected and unconventional; consumers are targeted in unexpected places, which can make the idea that's being marketed memorable, generate buzz, and even spread virally. The term was coined and defined by Jay Conrad Levinson in his 1984 book _____.
a. 1990 Clean Air Act
b. Relationship marketing
c. 28-hour day
d. Guerrilla marketing

7. _____ is an integrated communications-based process through which individuals and communities discover that existing and newly-identified needs and wants may be satisfied by the products and services of others.

_____ is defined by the American _____ Association as the activity, set of institutions, and processes for creating, communicating, delivering, and exchanging offerings that have value for customers, clients, partners, and society at large. The term developed from the original meaning which referred literally to going to market, as in shopping, or going to a market to buy or sell goods or services.

a. Marketing
b. Customer relationship management
c. Market development
d. Disruptive technology

8. A _____ is a form of qualitative research in which a group of people are asked about their attitude towards a product, service, concept, advertisement, idea, or packaging. Questions are asked in an interactive group setting where participants are free to talk with other group members.

The first _____s were created at the Bureau of Applied Social Research by associate director, sociologist Robert K. Merton.

a. Focus group
b. Market analysis
c. 1990 Clean Air Act
d. Marketing research

9. A _____ is a research instrument consisting of a series of questions and other prompts for the purpose of gathering information from respondents. Although they are often designed for statistical analysis of the responses, this is not always the case. The _____ was invented by Sir Francis Galton.
a. Structured interview
b. Questionnaire
c. Questionnaire construction
d. Mystery shoppers

10. An _____ is an organization founded and funded by businesses that operate in a specific industry. An industry trade association participates in public relations activities such as advertising, education, political donations, lobbying and publishing, but its main focus is collaboration between companies, or standardization. Associations may offer other services, such as producing conferences, networking or charitable events or offering classes or educational materials.
a. Industry trade group
b. A4e
c. AAAI
d. A Stake in the Outcome

Chapter 6. Conducting a Feasibility Analysis and Crafting a Winning Business Plan

11. In finance, the _____ or quick ratio or liquid ratio measures the ability of a company to use its near cash or quick assets to immediately extinguish or retire its current liabilities. Quick assets include those current assets that presumably can be quickly converted to cash at close to their book values.

Generally, the acid test ratio should be 1:1 or better, however this varies widely by industry.

   a. Inventory turnover
   b. Acid-test
   c. A4e
   d. A Stake in the Outcome

12. _____ or _____ data refers to selected population characteristics as used in government, marketing or opinion research, or the _____ profiles used in such research. Note the distinction from the term 'demography' Commonly-used _____ s include race, age, income, disabilities, mobility (in terms of travel time to work or number of vehicles available), educational attainment, home ownership, employment status, and even location.
   a. Affiliation
   b. Adam Smith
   c. Abraham Harold Maslow
   d. Demographic

13. Marketing research is a form of business research and is generally divided into two categories: consumer _____ and business-to-business (B2B) _____, which was previously known as industrial marketing research. Consumer marketing research studies the buying habits of individual people while business-to-business marketing research investigates the markets for products sold by one business to another.

Consumer _____ is a form of applied sociology that concentrates on understanding the behaviours, whims and preferences, of consumers in a market-based economy, and aims to understand the effects and comparative success of marketing campaigns.

   a. Questionnaire construction
   b. Mystery shoppers
   c. Questionnaire
   d. Market Research

14. The _____ is the Cabinet department of the United States government concerned with promoting economic growth. It was originally created as the _____ and Labor on February 14, 1903. It was subsequently renamed to the Department of Commerce on March 4, 1913, and its bureaus and agencies specializing in labor were transferred to the new Department of Labor.
   a. United States Department of Commerce
   b. AAAI
   c. A4e
   d. A Stake in the Outcome

15. Wholesaling, jobbing to industrial, commercial, institutional or to other _____ and related subordinated services.

According to the United Nations Statistics Division, 'wholesale' is the resale (sale without transformation) of new and used goods to retailers, to industrial, commercial, institutional or professional users or involves acting as an agent or broker in buying merchandise for such persons or companies. _____ frequently physically assemble, sort and grade goods in large lots, break bulk, repack and redistribute in smaller lots.

Chapter 6. Conducting a Feasibility Analysis and Crafting a Winning Business Plan 37

    a. Packaging
    b. Wholesalers
    c. Supply chain management
    d. Supply chain

16. A _____ is a business that is privately owned and operated, with a small number of employees and relatively low volume of sales. The legal definition of 'small' often varies by country and industry, but is generally under 100 employees in the United States and under 50 employees in the European Union. In comparison, the definition of mid-sized business by the number of employees is generally under 500 in the U.S. and 250 for the European Union.
    a. Golden Boot Compensation
    b. Pre-determined overhead rate
    c. Critical Success Factor
    d. Small Business

17. The _____ is a United States government agency that provides support to small businesses.

The mission of the _____ is 'to maintain and strengthen the nation's economy by enabling the establishment and viability of small businesses and by assisting in the economic recovery of communities after disasters.'

The _____ makes loans directly to businesses and acts as a guarantor on bank loans. In some circumstances it also makes loans to victims of natural disasters, works to get government procurement contracts for small businesses, and assists businesses with management, technical and training issues.

    a. 28-hour day
    b. 1990 Clean Air Act
    c. 33 Strategies of War
    d. Small Business Administration

18. _____ according to Onuoha (2007) is the practice of starting new organizations or revitalizing mature organizations, particularly new businesses generally in response to identified opportunities. _____ is often a difficult undertaking, as a vast majority of new businesses fail. Entrepreneurial activities are substantially different depending on the type of organization that is being started.
    a. A4e
    b. A Stake in the Outcome
    c. AAAI
    d. Entrepreneurship

19. A _____ is a brief written statement of the purpose of a company or organization. Ideally, a _____ guides the actions of the organization, spells out its overall goal, provides a sense of direction, and guides decision making for all levels of management.

_____ s often contain the following:

- Purpose and aim of the organization
- The organization's primary stakeholders: clients, stockholders, etc.
- Responsibilities of the organization toward these stakeholders
- Products and services offered

In developing a _____:

- Encourage as much input as feasible from employees, volunteers, and other stakeholders
- Publicize it broadly

Chapter 6. Conducting a Feasibility Analysis and Crafting a Winning Business Plan

The _____ can be used to resolve differences between business stakeholders. Stakeholders include: employees including managers and executives, stockholders, board of directors, customers, suppliers, distributors, creditors, governments (local, state, federal, etc.), unions, competitors, NGO's, and the general public.

a. 28-hour day
b. Mission statement
c. 1990 Clean Air Act
d. 33 Strategies of War

20. _____ refers to the aggregated strategies of single business firm or a strategic business unit (SBU) in a diversified corporation. According to Michael Porter, a firm must formulate a _____ that incorporates either cost leadership, differentiation or focus in order to achieve a sustainable competitive advantage and long-term success in its chosen arenas or industries.

Functional strategies include marketing strategies, new product development strategies, human resource strategies, financial strategies, legal strategies, supply-chain strategies, and information technology management strategies.

a. Business strategy
b. Strategic thinking
c. Competitive heterogeneity
d. Switching cost

21. A _____ is a written document that details the necessary actions to achieve one or more marketing objectives. It can be for a product or service, a brand, or a product line. _____s cover between one and five years.

a. Market development
b. Marketing plan
c. Disruptive technology
d. Marketing strategy

22. A _____ is a process that can allow an organization to concentrate its limited resources on the greatest opportunities to increase sales and achieve a sustainable competitive advantage. A _____ should be centered around the key concept that customer satisfaction is the main goal.

A _____ is a written plan which combines product development, promotion, distribution, and pricing approach, identifies the firm's marketing goals, and explains how they will be achieved within a stated timeframe.

a. Category management
b. Product bundling
c. Disruptive technology
d. Marketing strategy

23. In investing, financial markets are commonly believed to have _____ that can be classified as primary trends, secondary trends (short-term), and secular trends (long-term.) This belief is generally consistent with the non-scientific practice of technical analysis and broadly inconsistent with the standard academic view of financial markets, the efficient market hypothesis. The belief in trends incorporates the idea that market cycles occur with regularity and persistence.

a. 33 Strategies of War
b. 28-hour day
c. 1990 Clean Air Act
d. Market trends

24. The term '_____' refers to the concept of collecting information and attempting to spot a pattern in the information. In some fields of study, the term '_____' has more formally-defined meanings.

Chapter 6. Conducting a Feasibility Analysis and Crafting a Winning Business Plan

In project management _____ is a mathematical technique that uses historical results to predict future outcome.

a. Least squares
c. Regression analysis
b. Stepwise regression
d. Trend analysis

25. _____ in marketing and strategic management is an assessment of the strengths and weaknesses of current and potential competitors. This analysis provides both an offensive and defensive strategic context through which to identify opportunities and threats. Competitor profiling coalesces all of the relevant sources of _____ into one framework in the support of efficient and effective strategy formulation, implementation, monitoring and adjustment.

a. 28-hour day
c. Competitor or Competitive Intelligence
b. 1990 Clean Air Act
d. Competitor analysis

26. _____ is one of the four elements of marketing mix. An organization or set of organizations (go-betweens) involved in the process of making a product or service available for use or consumption by a consumer or business user.

The other three parts of the marketing mix are product, pricing, and promotion.

a. Missing completely at random
c. Distribution
b. Job creation programs
d. Matching theory

27. _____ is one of the four Ps of the marketing mix. The other three aspects are product, promotion, and place. It is also a key variable in microeconomic price allocation theory.

a. Price floor
c. Transfer pricing
b. Penetration pricing
d. Pricing

28. _____ are formal records of the financial activities of a business, person, or other entity. In British English, including United Kingdom company law, _____ are often referred to as accounts, although the term _____ is also used, particularly by accountants.

_____ provide an overview of a business or person's financial condition in both short and long term.

a. 33 Strategies of War
c. Financial statements
b. 28-hour day
d. 1990 Clean Air Act

29. An _____ is a person who has possession of an enterprise and assumes significant accountability for the inherent risks and the outcome. It is an ambitious leader who combines land, labor, and capital to create and market new goods or services. The term is a loanword from French and was first defined by the Irish economist Richard Cantillon.

a. A Stake in the Outcome
c. AAAI
b. A4e
d. Entrepreneur

30. In decision theory and estimation theory, the _____ of an estimator, $\hat{\theta}$, of an unknown parameter of the distribution, θ, is the expected value of the loss function

$$R(\theta, \hat{\theta}) = \mathbb{E}_\theta L(\theta, \hat{\theta}) = \int L(\theta, \hat{\theta}) \, dP_\theta.$$

where dP_θ is a probability measure parametrized by θ.

- For a scalar parameter θ and a quadratic loss function,

$$L(\theta, \hat{\theta}) = (\theta - \hat{\theta})^2$$

the _____ function becomes the mean squared error of the estimate,

$$R(\theta, \hat{\theta}) = E_\theta (\theta - \hat{\theta})^2$$

- In density estimation, the unknown parameter is probability density itself. The loss function is typically chosen to be a norm in an appropriate function space. For example, for L^2 norm,

$$L(f, \hat{f}) = \|f - \hat{f}\|_2^2$$

the _____ function becomes the mean integrated squared error

$$R(f, \hat{f}) = E\|f - \hat{f}\|^2$$

a. Financial modeling
b. Linear model
c. Risk aversion
d. Risk

31. An _____ is any party that makes an investment.

The term has taken on a specific meaning in finance to describe the particular types of people and companies that regularly purchase equity or debt securities for financial gain in exchange for funding an expanding company. Less frequently, the term is applied to parties who purchase real estate, currency, commodity derivatives, personal property, or other assets.

a. A4e
b. A Stake in the Outcome
c. AAAI
d. Investor

Chapter 7. Creating a Solid Financial Plan

1. In financial accounting, a _____ or statement of financial position is a summary of a person's or organization's balances. Assets, liabilities and ownership equity are listed as of a specific date, such as the end of its financial year. A _____ is often described as a snapshot of a company's financial condition.
   - a. 1990 Clean Air Act
   - b. 33 Strategies of War
   - c. 28-hour day
   - d. Balance sheet

2. _____ are formal records of the financial activities of a business, person, or other entity. In British English, including United Kingdom company law, _____ are often referred to as accounts, although the term _____ is also used, particularly by accountants.

   _____ provide an overview of a business or person's financial condition in both short and long term.

   - a. 33 Strategies of War
   - b. Financial statements
   - c. 1990 Clean Air Act
   - d. 28-hour day

3. In business and accounting, _____s are everything of value that is owned by a person or company. Any property or object of value that one possesses, usually considered as applicable to the payment of one's debts is considered an _____. Simplistically stated, _____s are things of value that can be readily converted into cash.
   - a. A4e
   - b. Asset
   - c. AAAI
   - d. A Stake in the Outcome

4. In accounting, a _____ is an asset on the balance sheet which is expected to be sold or otherwise used up in the near future, usually within one year, or one business cycle - whichever is longer. Typical _____s include cash, cash equivalents, accounts receivable, inventory, the portion of prepaid accounts which will be used within a year, and short-term investments.

   On the balance sheet, assets will typically be classified into _____s and long-term assets.

   - a. Net income
   - b. Matching principle
   - c. Treasury stock
   - d. Current asset

5. In finance, _____ are considered liabilities of the business that are to be settled in cash within the fiscal year or the operating cycle, whichever period is longer.

   For example accounts payable for goods, services or supplies that were purchased for use in the operation of the business and payable within a normal period of time would be _____.

   Bonds, mortgages and loans that are payable over a term exceeding one year would be fixed liabilities.

   - a. Current liabilities
   - b. Generally accepted accounting principles
   - c. Matching principle
   - d. Depreciation

6. _____ plant, and equipment, is a term used in accountancy for assets and property which cannot easily be converted into cash. This can be compared with current assets such as cash or bank accounts, which are described as liquid assets. In most cases, only tangible assets are referred to as fixed.

a. Fixed asset
c. 1990 Clean Air Act
b. 28-hour day
d. 33 Strategies of War

7. _____ are defined as identifiable non-monetary assets that cannot be seen, touched or physically measured, which are created through time and/or effort and that are identifiable as a separate asset. There are two primary forms of intangibles - legal intangibles (such as trade secrets (e.g., customer lists), copyrights, patents, trademarks, and goodwill) and competitive intangibles (such as knowledge activities (know-how, knowledge), collaboration activities, leverage activities, and structural activities.) Legal intangibles are known under the generic term intellectual property and generate legal property rights defensible in a court of law.
   a. Interlocking directorate
   b. Intangible assets
   c. Employee value proposition
   d. Induction programme

8. In economics, business, retail, and accounting, a _____ is the value of money that has been used up to produce something, and hence is not available for use anymore. In economics, a _____ is an alternative that is given up as a result of a decision. In business, the _____ may be one of acquisition, in which case the amount of money expended to acquire it is counted as _____.
   a. Fixed costs
   b. Cost overrun
   c. Cost allocation
   d. Cost

9. In financial accounting, _____ or cost of sales includes the direct costs attributable to the production of the goods sold by a company. This amount includes the materials cost used in creating the goods along with the direct labour costs used to produce the good. It excludes indirect expenses such as distribution costs and sales force costs.
   a. 1990 Clean Air Act
   b. 28-hour day
   c. Reorder point
   d. Cost of goods sold

10. In accounting, _____ or sales profit is the difference between revenue and the cost of making a product or providing a service, before deducting overhead, payroll, taxation, and interest payments. Note that this is different from operating profit (earnings before interest and taxes.)

Net sales are calculated:

   Net sales = Sales - Sales returns and allowances.

   a. Cash flow
   b. Gross profit margin
   c. Capital budgeting
   d. Gross profit

11. _____ is a financial ratio used to assess the profitability of a firm's core activities, excluding fixed costs.

The general calculation is:

The _____ is related to the net profit margin, which assesses the profitability of an organization after including fixed costs.

_____ indicates the relationship between net sales revenue and the cost of goods sold.

a. Sweat equity
c. Capital structure
b. Shareholder value
d. Gross profit margin

12. _____ is a company's financial statement that indicates how the revenue is transformed into the net income The purpose of the _____ is to show managers and investors whether the company made or lost money during the period being reported.

The important thing to remember about an _____ is that it represents a period of time.

a. Income statement
c. A Stake in the Outcome
b. AAAI
d. A4e

13. _____, net margin, net _____ or net profit ratio all refer to a measure of profitability. It is calculated by finding the net profit as a percentage of the revenue.

$$\text{Net profit margin} = \frac{\text{Net profit (after taxes)}}{\text{Revenue}} \times 100\%$$

The _____ is mostly used for internal comparison.

a. Profit maximization
c. 1990 Clean Air Act
b. Profit margin
d. Net profit margin

14. _____ is equal to the income that a firm has after subtracting costs and expenses from the total revenue. _____ can be distributed among holders of common stock as a dividend or held by the firm as retained earnings. _____ is an accounting term.

a. Generally accepted accounting principles
c. Net profit
b. Matching principle
d. Net income

15. An _____, operating expenditure, operational expense, operational expenditure or OPEX is an on-going cost for running a product, business, or system. Its counterpart, a capital expenditure (CAPEX), is the cost of developing or providing non-consumable parts for the product or system. For example, the purchase of a photocopier is the CAPEX, and the annual paper and toner cost is the OPEX.

a. A Stake in the Outcome
c. A4e
b. AAAI
d. Operating expense

16. _____ is a term used in accounting, economics and finance to spread the cost of an asset over the span of several years.

In simple words we can say that _____ is the reduction in the value of an asset due to usage, passage of time, wear and tear, technological outdating or obsolescence, depletion, inadequacy, rot, rust, decay or other such factors.

In accounting, _____ is a term used to describe any method of attributing the historical or purchase cost of an asset across its useful life, roughly corresponding to normal wear and tear.

   a. Net profit
   c. Matching principle
   b. Depreciation
   d. Treasury stock

17. In financial accounting, a cash flow statement or _____ is a financial statement that shows how changes in balance sheet and income accounts affect cash and cash equivalents, and breaks the analysis down to operating, investing, and financing activities. As an analytical tool, the _____ is useful in determining the short-term viability of a company, particularly its ability to pay bills. International Accounting Standard 7 (IAS 7), is the International Accounting Standard that deals with cash flow statements.

   a. Statement of cash flows
   c. 1990 Clean Air Act
   b. 33 Strategies of War
   d. 28-hour day

18. _____ refers to the movement of cash into or out of a business or financial product. It is usually measured during a specified, finite period of time. Measurement of _____ can be used

- to determine a project's rate of return or value. The time of _____s into and out of projects are used as inputs in financial models such as internal rate of return, and net present value.
- to determine problems with a business's liquidity. Being profitable does not necessarily mean being liquid. A company can fail because of a shortage of cash, even while profitable.
- as an alternate measure of a business's profits when it is believed that accrual accounting concepts do not represent economic realities. For example, a company may be notionally profitable but generating little operational cash (as may be the case for a company that barters its products rather than selling for cash.) In such a case, the company may be deriving additional operating cash by issuing shares evaluating default risk, re-investment requirements, etc.

_____ is a generic term used differently depending on the context. It may be defined by users for their own purposes.

   a. Gross profit margin
   c. Sweat equity
   b. Gross profit
   d. Cash flow

19. The _____ of an edge is $c_f(u,v) = c(u,v) - f(u,v)$. This defines a residual network denoted $G_f(V, E_f)$, giving the amount of available capacity. See that there can be an edge from u to v in the residual network, even though there is no edge from u to v in the original network.

   a. 33 Strategies of War
   c. 1990 Clean Air Act
   b. 28-hour day
   d. Residual capacity

20. A _____ is a business that is privately owned and operated, with a small number of employees and relatively low volume of sales. The legal definition of 'small' often varies by country and industry, but is generally under 100 employees in the United States and under 50 employees in the European Union. In comparison, the definition of mid-sized business by the number of employees is generally under 500 in the U.S. and 250 for the European Union.

a. Pre-determined overhead rate
b. Critical Success Factor
c. Small business
d. Golden Boot Compensation

21. _____ is the process of estimation in unknown situations. Prediction is a similar, but more general term. Both can refer to estimation of time series, cross-sectional or longitudinal data.

a. Forecasting
b. 1990 Clean Air Act
c. 28-hour day
d. 33 Strategies of War

22. The _____ is a United States government agency that provides support to small businesses.

The mission of the _____ is 'to maintain and strengthen the nation's economy by enabling the establishment and viability of small businesses and by assisting in the economic recovery of communities after disasters.'

The _____ makes loans directly to businesses and acts as a guarantor on bank loans. In some circumstances it also makes loans to victims of natural disasters, works to get government procurement contracts for small businesses, and assists businesses with management, technical and training issues.

a. 33 Strategies of War
b. 1990 Clean Air Act
c. 28-hour day
d. Small Business Administration

23. The _____ is a measure of how revenue growth translates into growth in operating income. It is a measure of leverage, and of how risky (volatile) a company's operating income is.

There are various measures of _____, which can be interpreted analogously to financial leverage.

a. A Stake in the Outcome
b. A4e
c. AAAI
d. Operating leverage

24. The _____ is a financial ratio that measures whether or not a firm has enough resources to pay its debts over the next 12 months. It compares a firm's current assets to its current liabilities. It is expressed as follows:

$$\text{Current ratio} = \frac{\text{Current Assets}}{\text{Current Liabilities}}$$

For example, if WXY Company's current assets are $50,000,000 and its current liabilities are $40,000,000, then its _____ would be $50,000,000 divided by $40,000,000, which equals 1.25.

a. Times interest earned
b. Return on assets
c. Financial ratio
d. Current ratio

25. Market _____ is a business, economics or investment term that refers to an asset's ability to be easily converted through an act of buying or selling without causing a significant movement in the price and with minimum loss of value. Money, or cash on hand, is the most liquid asset. An act of exchange of a less liquid asset with a more liquid asset is called liquidation.

a. Liquidity
b. 28-hour day
c. 33 Strategies of War
d. 1990 Clean Air Act

26. In finance, the _____ or quick ratio or liquid ratio measures the ability of a company to use its near cash or quick assets to immediately extinguish or retire its current liabilities. Quick assets include those current assets that presumably can be quickly converted to cash at close to their book values.

Generally, the acid test ratio should be 1:1 or better, however this varies widely by industry.

a. Inventory turnover
b. A Stake in the Outcome
c. A4e
d. Acid-test

27. _____ is a financial ratio that indicates the percentage of a company's assets are provided via debt. It is the ratio of total debt (the sum of current liabilities and long-term liabilities) and total assets (the sum of current assets, fixed assets, and other assets such as 'goodwill'.)

$$\text{Debt ratio} = \frac{\text{Total Debt}}{\text{Total Assets}}$$

or alternatively:

$$\text{Debt ratio} = \frac{\text{Total Liability}}{\text{Total Assets}}$$

For example, a company with $2 million in total assets and $500,000 in total liabilities would have a _____ of 25%

Like all financial ratios, a company's _____ should be compared with their industry average or other competing firms.

a. Demand forecasting
b. 28-hour day
c. 1990 Clean Air Act
d. Debt ratio

28. In finance, _____ is borrowing money to supplement existing funds for investment in such a way that the potential positive or negative outcome is magnified and/or enhanced. It generally refers to using borrowed funds, or debt, so as to attempt to increase the returns to equity. Deleveraging is the action of reducing borrowings.

a. Limited partners
b. Gearing
c. Limited liability corporation
d. Private equity

29. In business, _____ is the total liabilities minus total outside assets of an individual or a company. For a company, this is called shareholders' preference and may be referred to as book value. _____ is stated as at a particular year in time.

Chapter 7. Creating a Solid Financial Plan

a. Net worth
b. Novated lease
c. Deferred compensation
d. Payback period

30. _____ relates to the cost of borrowing money. It is the price that a lender charges a borrower for the use of the lender's money. _____ is different from OPEX and CAPEX, for it relates to the capital structure of a company.
   a. A Stake in the Outcome
   b. A4e
   c. Interest expense
   d. AAAI

31. The _____ is a financial term defined as a company's operating expenses as a percentage of revenue. This financial ratio is most commonly used for industries such as railroads which require a large percentage of revenues to maintain operations. In railroading, an _____ of 80 or lower is considered desirable.
   a. A4e
   b. AAAI
   c. A Stake in the Outcome
   d. Operating ratio

32. The _____ is an equation that equals the cost of goods sold divided by the average inventory. Average inventory equals beginning inventory plus ending inventory divided by 2.

The formula for _____:

The formula for average inventory:

A low turnover rate may point to overstocking, obsolescence, or deficiencies in the product line or marketing effort.

   a. A4e
   b. A Stake in the Outcome
   c. Inventory turnover
   d. Asset turnover

33. _____ is one of the Accounting Liquidity ratios, a financial ratio. This ratio measures the number of times, on average, the inventory is sold during the period. Its purpose is to measure the liquidity of the inventory.
   a. Inventory
   b. A4e
   c. A Stake in the Outcome
   d. Inventory turnover ratio

34. In a human resources context, _____ or labor _____ is the rate at which an employer gains and loses employees. Simple ways to describe it are 'how long employees tend to stay' or 'the rate of traffic through the revolving door.' _____ is measured for individual companies and for their industry as a whole. If an employer is said to have a high _____ relative to its competitors, it means that employees of that company have a shorter average tenure than those of other companies in the same industry.
   a. Ten year occupational employment projection
   b. Career portfolios
   c. Continuous
   d. Turnover

Chapter 7. Creating a Solid Financial Plan

35. In business and finance accounting, _____ is equal to the gross profit minus overheads minus interest payable plus/minus one off items for a given time period (usually: accounting period.)

A common synonym for '_____' when discussing financial statements (which include a balance sheet and an income statement) is the bottom line. This term results from the traditional appearance of an income statement which shows all allocated revenues and expenses over a specified time period with the resulting summation on the bottom line of the report.

a. Generally accepted accounting principles
b. Net profit
c. Matching principle
d. Treasury stock

36. The _____ percentage shows how profitable a company's assets are in generating revenue.

_____ can be computed as:

$$\text{ROA} = \frac{\text{Net Income} + \text{Interest Expense} - \text{Interest Tax savings}}{\text{Average Total Assets}}$$

This number tells you what the company can do with what it has, i.e. how many dollars of earnings they derive from each dollar of assets they control. Its a useful number for comparing competing companies in the same industry.

a. Return on Capital Employed
b. P/E ratio
c. Return on equity
d. Return on assets

37. In decision theory and estimation theory, the _____ of an estimator, $\hat{\theta}$, of an unknown parameter of the distribution, θ, is the expected value of the loss function

$$R(\theta, \hat{\theta}) = \mathbb{E}_\theta L(\theta, \hat{\theta}) = \int L(\theta, \hat{\theta}) \, dP_\theta.$$

Chapter 7. Creating a Solid Financial Plan

where dP_θ is a probability measure parametrized by θ.

- For a scalar parameter θ and a quadratic loss function,

$$L(\theta, \hat{\theta}) = (\theta - \hat{\theta})^2$$

the _____ function becomes the mean squared error of the estimate,

$$R(\theta, \hat{\theta}) = E_\theta (\theta - \hat{\theta})^2$$

- In density estimation, the unknown parameter is probability density itself. The loss function is typically chosen to be a norm in an appropriate function space. For example, for L^2 norm,

$$L(f, \hat{f}) = \|f - \hat{f}\|_2^2$$

the _____ function becomes the mean integrated squared error

$$R(f, \hat{f}) = E\|f - \hat{f}\|^2$$

a. Linear model
c. Financial modeling
b. Risk aversion
d. Risk

38. _____ is the identification, assessment, and prioritization of risks followed by coordinated and economical application of resources to minimize, monitor, and control the probability and/or impact of unfortunate events.. Risks can come from uncertainty in financial markets, project failures, legal liabilities, credit risk, accidents, natural causes and disasters as well as deliberate attacks from an adversary. Several _____ standards have been developed including the Project Management Institute, the National Institute of Science and Technology, actuarial societies, and ISO standards.
   a. Kanban
   b. Trademark
   c. Succession planning
   d. Risk Management

39. _____ is an advertisement in which a particular product specifically mentions a competitor by name for the express purpose of showing why the competitor is inferior to the product naming it.

This should not be confused with parody advertisements, where a fictional product is being advertised for the purpose of poking fun at the particular advertisement, nor should it be confused with the use of a coined brand name for the purpose of comparing the product without actually naming an actual competitor. ('Wikipedia tastes better and is less filling than the Encyclopedia Galactica.')

In the 1980s, during what has been referred to as the cola wars, soft-drink manufacturer Pepsi ran a series of advertisements where people, caught on hidden camera, in a blind taste test, chose Pepsi over rival Coca-Cola.

Chapter 7. Creating a Solid Financial Plan

a. 1990 Clean Air Act
b. 33 Strategies of War
c. 28-hour day
d. Comparative advertising

40. _____ is a mathematical science pertaining to the collection, analysis, interpretation or explanation, and presentation of data. It also provides tools for prediction and forecasting based on data. It is applicable to a wide variety of academic disciplines, from the natural and social sciences to the humanities, government and business.

a. Location parameter
b. Simple moving average
c. Statistics
d. Failure rate

41. The _____ is an independent agency of the United States government, established in 1914 by the _____ Act. Its principal mission is the promotion of 'consumer protection' and the elimination and prevention of what regulators perceive to be harmfully 'anti-competitive' business practices, such as coercive monopoly.

The _____ Act was one of President Wilson's major acts against trusts.

a. 33 Strategies of War
b. 28-hour day
c. 1990 Clean Air Act
d. Federal Trade Commission

42. The _____ was a regulatory body in the United States created by the Interstate Commerce Act of 1887, which was signed into law by President Grover Cleveland. The agency was abolished in 1995, and the agency's remaining functions were transferred to the Surface Transportation Board.

The Commission's five members were appointed by the President with the consent of the United States Senate.

a. Extended Enterprise
b. United States Department of Agriculture
c. American Institute of Industrial Engineers
d. Interstate Commerce Commission

43. The U.S. _____ is an independent agency of the United States government which holds primary responsibility for enforcing the federal securities laws and regulating the securities industry, the nation's stock and options exchanges, and other electronic securities markets. The SEC was created by section 4 of the Securities Exchange Act of 1934 (now codified as 15 U.S.C. § 78d and commonly referred to as the 1934 Act.)

a. 33 Strategies of War
b. 28-hour day
c. 1990 Clean Air Act
d. Securities and Exchange Commission

44. An _____ is an organization founded and funded by businesses that operate in a specific industry. An industry trade association participates in public relations activities such as advertising, education, political donations, lobbying and publishing, but its main focus is collaboration between companies, or standardization. Associations may offer other services, such as producing conferences, networking or charitable events or offering classes or educational materials.

a. AAAI
b. A4e
c. A Stake in the Outcome
d. Industry trade group

45. The _____ is the Cabinet department of the United States government concerned with promoting economic growth. It was originally created as the _____ and Labor on February 14, 1903. It was subsequently renamed to the Department of Commerce on March 4, 1913, and its bureaus and agencies specializing in labor were transferred to the new Department of Labor.

a. United States Department of Commerce
b. A Stake in the Outcome
c. AAAI
d. A4e

46. The term '_____' refers to the concept of collecting information and attempting to spot a pattern in the information. In some fields of study, the term '_____' has more formally-defined meanings.

In project management _____ is a mathematical technique that uses historical results to predict future outcome.

a. Regression analysis
b. Stepwise regression
c. Trend analysis
d. Least squares

Chapter 8. Managing Cash Flow

1. _____ refers to the movement of cash into or out of a business or financial product. It is usually measured during a specified, finite period of time. Measurement of _____ can be used

    - to determine a project's rate of return or value. The time of _____s into and out of projects are used as inputs in financial models such as internal rate of return, and net present value.
    - to determine problems with a business's liquidity. Being profitable does not necessarily mean being liquid. A company can fail because of a shortage of cash, even while profitable.
    - as an alternate measure of a business's profits when it is believed that accrual accounting concepts do not represent economic realities. For example, a company may be notionally profitable but generating little operational cash (as may be the case for a company that barters its products rather than selling for cash.) In such a case, the company may be deriving additional operating cash by issuing shares evaluating default risk, re-investment requirements, etc.

    _____ is a generic term used differently depending on the context. It may be defined by users for their own purposes.

    a. Sweat equity
    c. Gross profit margin
    b. Gross profit
    d. Cash flow

2. _____ is one of the managerial functions like planning, organizing, staffing and directing. It is an important function because it helps to check the errors and to take the corrective action so that deviation from standards are minimized and stated goals of the organization are achieved in desired manner. According to modern concepts, _____ is a foreseeing action whereas earlier concept of _____ was used only when errors were detected. _____ in management means setting standards, measuring actual performance and taking corrective action.
    a. Control
    c. Schedule of reinforcement
    b. Decision tree pruning
    d. Turnover

3. An _____ is a person who has possession of an enterprise and assumes significant accountability for the inherent risks and the outcome. It is an ambitious leader who combines land, labor, and capital to create and market new goods or services. The term is a loanword from French and was first defined by the Irish economist Richard Cantillon.
    a. A Stake in the Outcome
    c. AAAI
    b. Entrepreneur
    d. A4e

4. In economics, business, retail, and accounting, a _____ is the value of money that has been used up to produce something, and hence is not available for use anymore. In economics, a _____ is an alternative that is given up as a result of a decision. In business, the _____ may be one of acquisition, in which case the amount of money expended to acquire it is counted as _____.
    a. Cost allocation
    c. Fixed costs
    b. Cost
    d. Cost overrun

5. In business, overhead, _____ or overhead expense refers to an ongoing expense of operating a business. The term overhead is usually used to group expenses that are necessary to the continued functioning of the business, but do not directly generate profits.

Overhead expenses are all costs on the income statement except for direct labor and direct materials.

Chapter 8. Managing Cash Flow

a. Industrial market segmentation
c. Intangible assets
b. Interlocking directorate
d. Overhead cost

6. _____ is an advertisement in which a particular product specifically mentions a competitor by name for the express purpose of showing why the competitor is inferior to the product naming it.

This should not be confused with parody advertisements, where a fictional product is being advertised for the purpose of poking fun at the particular advertisement, nor should it be confused with the use of a coined brand name for the purpose of comparing the product without actually naming an actual competitor. ('Wikipedia tastes better and is less filling than the Encyclopedia Galactica.')

In the 1980s, during what has been referred to as the cola wars, soft-drink manufacturer Pepsi ran a series of advertisements where people, caught on hidden camera, in a blind taste test, chose Pepsi over rival Coca-Cola.

a. 1990 Clean Air Act
c. 33 Strategies of War
b. Comparative advertising
d. 28-hour day

7. _____ generally refers to a list of all planned expenses and revenues. It is a plan for saving and spending. A _____ is an important concept in microeconomics, which uses a _____ line to illustrate the trade-offs between two or more goods.
a. Budget
c. 1990 Clean Air Act
b. 33 Strategies of War
d. 28-hour day

8. _____ is a form of communication that typically attempts to persuade potential customers to purchase or to consume more of a particular brand of product or service. 'While now central to the contemporary global economy and the reproduction of global production networks, it is only quite recently that _____ has been more than a marginal influence on patterns of sales and production. The formation of modern _____ was intimately bound up with the emergence of new forms of monopoly capitalism around the end of the 19th and beginning of the 20th century as one element in corporate strategies to create, organize and where possible control markets, especially for mass produced consumer goods.
a. A4e
c. AAAI
b. A Stake in the Outcome
d. Advertising

9. _____ is the process of estimation in unknown situations. Prediction is a similar, but more general term. Both can refer to estimation of time series, cross-sectional or longitudinal data.
a. 28-hour day
c. 33 Strategies of War
b. 1990 Clean Air Act
d. Forecasting

10. _____ is one of a series of accounting transactions dealing with the billing of customers who owe money to a person, company or organization for goods and services that have been provided to the customer. In most business entities this is typically done by generating an invoice and mailing or electronically delivering it to the customer, who in turn must pay it within an established timeframe called credit or payment terms.

An example of a common payment term is Net 30, meaning payment is due in the amount of the invoice 30 days from the date of invoice.

a. Accounts receivable
c. Other revenue
b. Accumulated Depreciation
d. A Stake in the Outcome

11. A _____ is typically described as a deliberate plan of action to guide decisions and achieve rational outcome(s.) However, the term may also be used to denote what is actually done, even though it is unplanned.

The term may apply to government, private sector organizations and groups, and individuals.

a. 1990 Clean Air Act
c. Policy
b. 28-hour day
d. 33 Strategies of War

12. In decision theory and estimation theory, the _____ of an estimator, $\hat{\theta}$, of an unknown parameter of the distribution, θ, is the expected value of the loss function

$$R(\theta, \hat{\theta}) = \mathbb{E}_\theta L(\theta, \hat{\theta}) = \int L(\theta, \hat{\theta})\, dP_\theta.$$

where dP_θ is a probability measure parametrized by θ.

- For a scalar parameter θ and a quadratic loss function,

$$L(\theta, \hat{\theta}) = (\theta - \hat{\theta})^2$$

the _____ function becomes the mean squared error of the estimate,

$$R(\theta, \hat{\theta}) = E_\theta(\theta - \hat{\theta})^2$$

- In density estimation, the unknown parameter is probability density itself. The loss function is typically chosen to be a norm in an appropriate function space. For example, for L^2 norm,

$$L(f, \hat{f}) = \|f - \hat{f}\|_2^2$$

the _____ function becomes the mean integrated squared error

$$R(f, \hat{f}) = E\|f - \hat{f}\|^2$$

a. Linear model
c. Risk aversion
b. Financial modeling
d. Risk

Chapter 8. Managing Cash Flow

13. _____-model (SCOR(r)) is a process reference model developed by the management consulting firm PRTM and AMR Research and endorsed by the Supply-Chain Council (SCC) as the cross-industry de facto standard diagnostic tool for supply chain management. SCOR enables users to address, improve, and communicate supply chain management practices within and between all interested parties in the Extended Enterprise.

SCOR(r) is a management tool, spanning from the supplier's supplier to the customer's customer. The model has been developed by the members of the Council on a volunteer basis to describe the business activities associated with all phases of satisfying a customer's demand.

a. Supply chain management software
b. Supply-Chain Operations Reference
c. Delayed differentiation
d. Supply Chain Risk Management

14. A _____ is a business that is privately owned and operated, with a small number of employees and relatively low volume of sales. The legal definition of 'small' often varies by country and industry, but is generally under 100 employees in the United States and under 50 employees in the European Union. In comparison, the definition of mid-sized business by the number of employees is generally under 500 in the U.S. and 250 for the European Union.

a. Critical Success Factor
b. Small Business
c. Pre-determined overhead rate
d. Golden Boot Compensation

15. _____ is the practice of managing the flow of information between an organization and its publics. _____ gains an organization or individual exposure to their audiences using topics of public interest and news items that do not require direct payment. Because _____ places exposure in credible third-party outlets, it offers a third-party legitimacy that advertising does not have.

a. 1990 Clean Air Act
b. Two-way communication
c. 28-hour day
d. Public Relations

16. _____ is a file or account that contains money that a person or company owes to suppliers, but has not paid yet (a form of debt.) When you receive an invoice you add it to the file, and then you remove it when you pay. Thus, the A/P is a form of credit that suppliers offer to their purchasers by allowing them to pay for a product or service after it has already been received.

a. Accounts receivable
b. Other revenue
c. Accounts payable
d. A Stake in the Outcome

17. The _____, first published in 1952, is one of a number of uniform acts that have been promulgated in conjunction with efforts to harmonize the law of sales and other commercial transactions in all 50 states within the United States of America. This objective is deemed important because of the prevalence of commercial transactions that extend beyond one state (for example, where the goods are manufactured in state A, warehoused in state B, sold from state C and delivered in state D.) The _____ deals primarily with transactions involving personal property (movable property), not real property (immovable property.)

a. Uniform Commercial Code
b. AAAI
c. A Stake in the Outcome
d. A4e

18. _____ , also referred to simply as a 'public offering' or 'flotation,' is when a company issues common stock or shares to the public for the first time. They are often issued by smaller, younger companies seeking capital to expand, but can also be done by large privately-owned companies looking to become publicly traded.

In an _____ the issuer may obtain the assistance of an underwriting firm, which helps it determine what type of security to issue (common or preferred), best offering price and time to bring it to market.

a. Outsourcing
b. Unemployment insurance
c. Occupational Safety and Health Administration
d. Initial public offering

19. _____ is subcontracting a process, such as product design or manufacturing, to a third-party company. The decision to outsource is often made in the interest of lowering cost or making better use of time and energy costs, redirecting or conserving energy directed at the competencies of a particular business, or to make more efficient use of land, labor, capital, (information) technology and resources. _____ became part of the business lexicon during the 1980s.

a. Unemployment insurance
b. Operant conditioning
c. Outsourcing
d. Opinion leadership

20. The phrase mergers and _____s refers to the aspect of corporate strategy, corporate finance and management dealing with the buying, selling and combining of different companies that can aid, finance, or help a growing company in a given industry grow rapidly without having to create another business entity.

An _____, also known as a takeover or a buyout, is the buying of one company (the 'target') by another. An _____ may be friendly or hostile.

a. A Stake in the Outcome
b. Acquisition
c. A4e
d. AAAI

21. _____ is a technique of planning and decision-making which reverses the working process of traditional budgeting. In traditional incremental budgeting, departmental managers justify only increases over the previous year budget and what has been already spent is automatically sanctioned. No reference is made to the previous level of expenditure.

a. 33 Strategies of War
b. 28-hour day
c. Zero-based budgeting
d. 1990 Clean Air Act

22. _____, commonly known as e-commerce, consists of the buying and selling of products or services over electronic systems such as the Internet and other computer networks. The amount of trade conducted electronically has grown extraordinarily with widespread Internet usage. The use of commerce is conducted in this way, spurring and drawing on innovations in electronic funds transfer, supply chain management, Internet marketing, online transaction processing, electronic data interchange (EDI), inventory management systems, and automated data collection systems.

a. Online shopping
b. A Stake in the Outcome
c. A4e
d. Electronic Commerce

23. A _____ is a formal statement of a set of business goals, the reasons why they are believed attainable, and the plan for reaching those goals. It may also contain background information about the organization or team attempting to reach those goals.

The business goals may be defined for for-profit or for non-profit organizations.

a. Distributed management
c. Time management
b. Business plan
d. Crisis management

Chapter 9. Building a Guerrilla Marketing Plan

1. _____ is an unconventional system of promotions that relies on time, energy and imagination rather than a big marketing budget. Typically, _____ tactics are unexpected and unconventional; consumers are targeted in unexpected places, which can make the idea that's being marketed memorable, generate buzz, and even spread virally. The term was coined and defined by Jay Conrad Levinson in his 1984 book _____.
   a. Guerrilla marketing
   b. Relationship marketing
   c. 28-hour day
   d. 1990 Clean Air Act

2. _____ is an integrated communications-based process through which individuals and communities discover that existing and newly-identified needs and wants may be satisfied by the products and services of others.

   _____ is defined by the American _____ Association as the activity, set of institutions, and processes for creating, communicating, delivering, and exchanging offerings that have value for customers, clients, partners, and society at large. The term developed from the original meaning which referred literally to going to market, as in shopping, or going to a market to buy or sell goods or services.

   a. Marketing
   b. Market development
   c. Customer relationship management
   d. Disruptive technology

3. A _____ is a written document that details the necessary actions to achieve one or more marketing objectives. It can be for a product or service, a brand, or a product line. _____s cover between one and five years.
   a. Marketing strategy
   b. Market development
   c. Disruptive technology
   d. Marketing plan

4. Marketing research is a form of business research and is generally divided into two categories: consumer _____ and business-to-business (B2B) _____, which was previously known as industrial marketing research. Consumer marketing research studies the buying habits of individual people while business-to-business marketing research investigates the markets for products sold by one business to another.

   Consumer _____ is a form of applied sociology that concentrates on understanding the behaviours, whims and preferences, of consumers in a market-based economy, and aims to understand the effects and comparative success of marketing campaigns.

   a. Questionnaire construction
   b. Mystery shoppers
   c. Market research
   d. Questionnaire

5. _____ is the process of extracting hidden patterns from data. As more data is gathered, with the amount of data doubling every three years, _____ is becoming an increasingly important tool to transform this data into information. It is commonly used in a wide range of profiling practices, such as marketing, surveillance, fraud detection and scientific discovery.
   a. 28-hour day
   b. Decision tree learning
   c. 1990 Clean Air Act
   d. Data mining

6. _____ or _____ data refers to selected population characteristics as used in government, marketing or opinion research, or the _____ profiles used in such research. Note the distinction from the term 'demography' Commonly-used _____s include race, age, income, disabilities, mobility (in terms of travel time to work or number of vehicles available), educational attainment, home ownership, employment status, and even location.

a. Abraham Harold Maslow
c. Affiliation

b. Adam Smith
d. Demographic

7. _____ is a form of marketing developed from direct response marketing campaigns conducted in the 1970s and 1980s which emphasizes customer retention and satisfaction, rather than a dominant focus on point-of-sale transactions.

_____ differs from other forms of marketing in that it recognizes the long term value to the firm of keeping customers, as opposed to direct or 'Intrusion' marketing, which focuses upon acquisition of new clients by targeting majority demographics based upon prospective client lists.

_____ refers to a long-term and mutually beneficial arrangement wherein both the buyer and seller focus on value enhancement with the goal of providing a more satisfying exchange.

a. 28-hour day
c. Guerrilla marketing

b. 1990 Clean Air Act
d. Relationship marketing

8. In decision theory and estimation theory, the _____ of an estimator, $\hat{\theta}$, of an unknown parameter of the distribution, θ, is the expected value of the loss function

$$R(\theta, \hat{\theta}) = \mathbb{E}_\theta L(\theta, \hat{\theta}) = \int L(\theta, \hat{\theta})\, dP_\theta.$$

where dP_θ is a probability measure parametrized by θ.

- For a scalar parameter θ and a quadratic loss function,

$$L(\theta, \hat{\theta}) = (\theta - \hat{\theta})^2$$

the _____ function becomes the mean squared error of the estimate,

$$R(\theta, \hat{\theta}) = E_\theta(\theta - \hat{\theta})^2$$

- In density estimation, the unknown parameter is probability density itself. The loss function is typically chosen to be a norm in an appropriate function space. For example, for L^2 norm,

$$L(f, \hat{f}) = \|f - \hat{f}\|_2^2$$

the _____ function becomes the mean integrated squared error

$$R(f, \hat{f}) = E\|f - \hat{f}\|^2$$

a. Financial modeling
c. Risk aversion
b. Linear model
d. Risk

9. _____ is the activity that the selling organization undertakes to reduce customer account defections. The success of this activity is when the customer account places an additional order before a 12-month period has expired. Note that ideally these orders will need to contribute similar financial amounts to the previous 12 months.

a. Business rule
c. Customer retention
b. Process automation
d. Foreign ownership

10. _____ is a business management strategy, initially implemented by Motorola, that today enjoys widespread application in many sectors of industry.

_____ seeks to improve the quality of process outputs by identifying and removing the causes of defects (errors) and variation in manufacturing and business processes. It uses a set of quality management methods, including statistical methods, and creates a special infrastructure of people within the organization ('Black Belts' etc.)

a. Takt time
c. Theory of constraints
b. Production line
d. Six Sigma

Chapter 9. Building a Guerrilla Marketing Plan 61

11. _____ is a business management strategy aimed at embedding awareness of quality in all organizational processes. _____ has been widely used in manufacturing, education, hospitals, call centers, government, and service industries, as well as NASA space and science programs.

As defined by the International Organization for Standardization (ISO):

'_____ is a management approach for an organization, centered on quality, based on the participation of all its members and aiming at long-term success through customer satisfaction, and benefits to all members of the organization and to society.' ISO 8402:1994

One major aim is to reduce variation from every process so that greater consistency of effort is obtained. (Royse, D., Thyer, B., Padgett D., ' Logan T., 2006)

a. 1990 Clean Air Act
c. 28-hour day
b. Quality management
d. Total quality management

12. _____ can be considered to have three main components: quality control, quality assurance and quality improvement. _____ is focused not only on product quality, but also the means to achieve it. _____ therefore uses quality assurance and control of processes as well as products to achieve more consistent quality.

a. Quality management
c. 1990 Clean Air Act
b. 28-hour day
d. Total quality management

13. In business and engineering, new _____ is the term used to describe the complete process of bringing a new product or service to market. There are two parallel paths involved in the NProduct development process: one involves the idea generation, product design, and detail engineering; the other involves market research and marketing analysis. Companies typically see new _____ as the first stage in generating and commercializing new products within the overall strategic process of product life cycle management used to maintain or grow their market share.

a. 33 Strategies of War
c. 28-hour day
b. 1990 Clean Air Act
d. Product Development

14. _____, a business term, is a measure of how products and services supplied by a company meet or surpass customer expectation. It is seen as a key performance indicator within business and is part of the four perspectives of a Balanced Scorecard.

In a competitive marketplace where businesses compete for customers, _____ is seen as a key differentiator and increasingly has become a key element of business strategy.

a. Horizontal integration
c. Customer satisfaction
b. Critical Success Factor
d. Foreign ownership

15. _____ is an advertisement in which a particular product specifically mentions a competitor by name for the express purpose of showing why the competitor is inferior to the product naming it.

Chapter 9. Building a Guerrilla Marketing Plan

This should not be confused with parody advertisements, where a fictional product is being advertised for the purpose of poking fun at the particular advertisement, nor should it be confused with the use of a coined brand name for the purpose of comparing the product without actually naming an actual competitor. ('Wikipedia tastes better and is less filling than the Encyclopedia Galactica.')

In the 1980s, during what has been referred to as the cola wars, soft-drink manufacturer Pepsi ran a series of advertisements where people, caught on hidden camera, in a blind taste test, chose Pepsi over rival Coca-Cola.

a. 33 Strategies of War
b. 1990 Clean Air Act
c. Comparative advertising
d. 28-hour day

16. _____, commonly known as e-commerce, consists of the buying and selling of products or services over electronic systems such as the Internet and other computer networks. The amount of trade conducted electronically has grown extraordinarily with widespread Internet usage. The use of commerce is conducted in this way, spurring and drawing on innovations in electronic funds transfer, supply chain management, Internet marketing, online transaction processing, electronic data interchange (EDI), inventory management systems, and automated data collection systems.

a. A4e
b. Online shopping
c. A Stake in the Outcome
d. Electronic Commerce

17. _____-model (SCOR(r)) is a process reference model developed by the management consulting firm PRTM and AMR Research and endorsed by the Supply-Chain Council (SCC) as the cross-industry de facto standard diagnostic tool for supply chain management. SCOR enables users to address, improve, and communicate supply chain management practices within and between all interested parties in the Extended Enterprise.

SCOR(r) is a management tool, spanning from the supplier's supplier to the customer's customer. The model has been developed by the members of the Council on a volunteer basis to describe the business activities associated with all phases of satisfying a customer's demand.

a. Supply Chain Risk Management
b. Supply-Chain Operations Reference
c. Supply chain management software
d. Delayed differentiation

18. _____ is a worldwide management consulting firm that focuses on solving issues of concern to senior management. McKinsey serves as an advisor to the world's leading businesses, governments, and institutions. It is widely recognized as a leader and one of the most prestigious firms in the management consulting industry.

a. 1990 Clean Air Act
b. 28-hour day
c. McKinsey ' Company
d. 33 Strategies of War

19. A _____ is a name or trademark connected with a product or producer. _____s have become increasingly important components of culture and the economy, now being described as 'cultural accessories and personal philosophies'.

Some people distinguish the psychological aspect of a _____ from the experiential aspect.

a. Brand awareness
b. Brand extension
c. Brand loyalty
d. Brand

20. The _____ is generally accepted as the use and specification of the 'four P's' describing the strategic position of a product in the marketplace. One version of the _____ originated in 1948 when James Culliton said that a marketing decision should be a result of something similar to a recipe. This version was used in 1953 when Neil Borden, in his American Marketing Association presidential address, took the recipe idea one step further and coined the term 'marketing-mix'.

a. 1990 Clean Air Act
b. 28-hour day
c. 33 Strategies of War
d. Marketing mix

21. _____ Management is the succession of strategies used by management as a product goes through its _____. The conditions in which a product is sold changes over time and must be managed as it moves through its succession of stages.

The _____ goes through many phases, involves many professional disciplines, and requires many skills, tools and processes.

a. Strategic Alliance
b. Golden handshake
c. Product life cycle
d. Job hunting

22. _____ is one of the four elements of marketing mix. An organization or set of organizations (go-betweens) involved in the process of making a product or service available for use or consumption by a consumer or business user.

The other three parts of the marketing mix are product, pricing, and promotion.

a. Matching theory
b. Missing completely at random
c. Job creation programs
d. Distribution

23. _____ is one of a series of accounting transactions dealing with the billing of customers who owe money to a person, company or organization for goods and services that have been provided to the customer. In most business entities this is typically done by generating an invoice and mailing or electronically delivering it to the customer, who in turn must pay it within an established timeframe called credit or payment terms.

An example of a common payment term is Net 30, meaning payment is due in the amount of the invoice 30 days from the date of invoice.

a. Accounts receivable
b. A Stake in the Outcome
c. Accumulated Depreciation
d. Other revenue

Chapter 10. Creative Use of Advertising and Promotion

1. _____ is a form of communication that typically attempts to persuade potential customers to purchase or to consume more of a particular brand of product or service. 'While now central to the contemporary global economy and the reproduction of global production networks, it is only quite recently that _____ has been more than a marginal influence on patterns of sales and production. The formation of modern _____ was intimately bound up with the emergence of new forms of monopoly capitalism around the end of the 19th and beginning of the 20th century as one element in corporate strategies to create, organize and where possible control markets, especially for mass produced consumer goods.
   a. A4e
   b. Advertising
   c. A Stake in the Outcome
   d. AAAI

2. The _____ is a marketing concept that was first proposed as a theory to explain a pattern among successful advertising campaigns of the early 1940s. It states that such campaigns made unique propositions to the customer and that this convinced them to switch brands. The term was invented by Rosser Reeves of Ted Bates ' Company.
   a. Unique selling proposition
   b. AAAI
   c. A Stake in the Outcome
   d. A4e

3. _____ , also referred to simply as a 'public offering' or 'flotation,' is when a company issues common stock or shares to the public for the first time. They are often issued by smaller, younger companies seeking capital to expand, but can also be done by large privately-owned companies looking to become publicly traded.

   In an _____ the issuer may obtain the assistance of an underwriting firm, which helps it determine what type of security to issue (common or preferred), best offering price and time to bring it to market.

   a. Outsourcing
   b. Occupational Safety and Health Administration
   c. Unemployment insurance
   d. Initial public offering

4. In economics, business, retail, and accounting, a _____ is the value of money that has been used up to produce something, and hence is not available for use anymore. In economics, a _____ is an alternative that is given up as a result of a decision. In business, the _____ may be one of acquisition, in which case the amount of money expended to acquire it is counted as _____.
   a. Cost allocation
   b. Fixed costs
   c. Cost overrun
   d. Cost

5. A _____ is a group of people or organizations sharing one or more characteristics that cause them to have similar product and/or service needs. A true _____ meets all of the following criteria: it is distinct from other segments (different segments have different needs), it is homogeneous within the segment (exhibits common needs); it responds similarly to a market stimulus, and it can be reached by a market intervention. The term is also used when consumers with identical product and/or service needs are divided up into groups so they can be charged different amounts.
   a. Market segment
   b. Customer relationship management
   c. SWOT analysis
   d. Context analysis

6. _____ are long-format television commercials, typically five minutes or longer.. _____ are also known as paid programming (or teleshopping in Europe.) Originally, they were a phenomenon that started in the United States where they were typically shown overnight (usually 2:00 a.m. to 6:00 a.m.)
   a. A Stake in the Outcome
   b. A4e
   c. AAAI
   d. Infomercials

Chapter 10. Creative Use of Advertising and Promotion

7. _____ systems are rule-based systems that are able to automatically provide solutions to repetitive management problems (Turban, Leidner, McLean and Wetherbe, 2007.) _____s are very closely related to business informatics and business analytics.

_____ systems are based on business rules.

a. Efficient Consumer Response
b. Entertainment Management
c. Executive development
d. Automated decision support

8. A _____ is a business that is privately owned and operated, with a small number of employees and relatively low volume of sales. The legal definition of 'small' often varies by country and industry, but is generally under 100 employees in the United States and under 50 employees in the European Union. In comparison, the definition of mid-sized business by the number of employees is generally under 500 in the U.S. and 250 for the European Union.

a. Golden Boot Compensation
b. Pre-determined overhead rate
c. Critical Success Factor
d. Small Business

9. _____ is an integrated communications-based process through which individuals and communities discover that existing and newly-identified needs and wants may be satisfied by the products and services of others.

_____ is defined by the American _____ Association as the activity, set of institutions, and processes for creating, communicating, delivering, and exchanging offerings that have value for customers, clients, partners, and society at large. The term developed from the original meaning which referred literally to going to market, as in shopping, or going to a market to buy or sell goods or services.

a. Market development
b. Customer relationship management
c. Disruptive technology
d. Marketing

10. _____ is an advertisement in which a particular product specifically mentions a competitor by name for the express purpose of showing why the competitor is inferior to the product naming it.

This should not be confused with parody advertisements, where a fictional product is being advertised for the purpose of poking fun at the particular advertisement, nor should it be confused with the use of a coined brand name for the purpose of comparing the product without actually naming an actual competitor. ('Wikipedia tastes better and is less filling than the Encyclopedia Galactica.')

In the 1980s, during what has been referred to as the cola wars, soft-drink manufacturer Pepsi ran a series of advertisements where people, caught on hidden camera, in a blind taste test, chose Pepsi over rival Coca-Cola.

a. 28-hour day
b. 1990 Clean Air Act
c. 33 Strategies of War
d. Comparative advertising

11. Consumer market research is a form of applied sociology that concentrates on understanding the behaviours, whims and preferences, of consumers in a market-based economy, and aims to understand the effects and comparative success of marketing campaigns. The field of consumer _____ as a statistical science was pioneered by Arthur Nielsen with the founding of the ACNielsen Company in 1923 .

Thus _____ is the systematic and objective identification, collection, analysis, and dissemination of information for the purpose of assisting management in decision making related to the identification and solution of problems and opportunities in marketing.

a. Market analysis
b. 1990 Clean Air Act
c. Marketing research process
d. Marketing Research

12. In the field of human resource management, _____ is the field concerned with organizational activity aimed at bettering the performance of individuals and groups in organizational settings. It has been known by several names, including employee development, human resource development, and learning and development.

Harrison observes that the name was endlessly debated by the Chartered Institute of Personnel and Development during its review of professional standards in 1999/2000.

a. Revolving door syndrome
b. Person specification
c. Training and Development
d. Performance appraisal

13. _____ generally refers to a list of all planned expenses and revenues. It is a plan for saving and spending. A _____ is an important concept in microeconomics, which uses a _____ line to illustrate the trade-offs between two or more goods.

a. 1990 Clean Air Act
b. 33 Strategies of War
c. 28-hour day
d. Budget

14. _____ or cause-related marketing refers to a type of marketing involving the cooperative efforts of a 'for profit' business and a non-profit organization for mutual benefit. The term is sometimes used more broadly and generally to refer to any type of marketing effort for social and other charitable causes, including in-house marketing efforts by non-profit organizations. _____ differs from corporate giving (philanthropy) as the latter generally involves a specific donation that is tax deductible, while _____ is a marketing relationship generally not based on a donation.

a. Relationship marketing
b. 1990 Clean Air Act
c. 28-hour day
d. Cause marketing

Chapter 11. Pricing and Credit Strategies

1. _____ is one of the four Ps of the marketing mix. The other three aspects are product, promotion, and place. It is also a key variable in microeconomic price allocation theory.
   a. Price floor
   b. Penetration pricing
   c. Transfer pricing
   d. Pricing

2. _____ is one of a series of accounting transactions dealing with the billing of customers who owe money to a person, company or organization for goods and services that have been provided to the customer. In most business entities this is typically done by generating an invoice and mailing or electronically delivering it to the customer, who in turn must pay it within an established timeframe called credit or payment terms.

   An example of a common payment term is Net 30, meaning payment is due in the amount of the invoice 30 days from the date of invoice.

   a. A Stake in the Outcome
   b. Accounts receivable
   c. Accumulated Depreciation
   d. Other revenue

3. A _____ is a government imposed limit on how high a price can be charged on a product. _____s are often intended to protect consumers from certain conditions that could make necessities unattainable. But they can also cause problems if they are used for a prolonged period of time without controlled rationing.
   a. Price points
   b. Price ceiling
   c. Price floor
   d. Price discrimination

4. In economics, business, retail, and accounting, a _____ is the value of money that has been used up to produce something, and hence is not available for use anymore. In economics, a _____ is an alternative that is given up as a result of a decision. In business, the _____ may be one of acquisition, in which case the amount of money expended to acquire it is counted as _____.
   a. Fixed costs
   b. Cost overrun
   c. Cost allocation
   d. Cost

5. In marketing a _____ is a ticket or document that can be exchanged for a financial discount or rebate when purchasing a product. Customarily, _____s are issued by manufacturers of consumer packaged goods or by retailers, to be used in retail stores as a part of sales promotions. They are often widely distributed through mail, magazines, newspapers, the Internet, and mobile devices such as cell phones.
   a. 1990 Clean Air Act
   b. Sales promotion
   c. Word of mouth
   d. Coupon

6. _____ or promotional products refers to articles of merchandise that are used in marketing and communication programs. These items are usually imprinted with a company's name, logo or slogan, and given away at trade shows, conferences, and as part of guerrilla marketing campaigns.

   Almost anything can be branded with a company's name or logo and used for promotion.

   a. Promotional items
   b. 33 Strategies of War
   c. 1990 Clean Air Act
   d. 28-hour day

Chapter 11. Pricing and Credit Strategies

7. _____ is a form of communication that typically attempts to persuade potential customers to purchase or to consume more of a particular brand of product or service. 'While now central to the contemporary global economy and the reproduction of global production networks, it is only quite recently that _____ has been more than a marginal influence on patterns of sales and production. The formation of modern _____ was intimately bound up with the emergence of new forms of monopoly capitalism around the end of the 19th and beginning of the 20th century as one element in corporate strategies to create, organize and where possible control markets, especially for mass produced consumer goods.

   a. AAAI
   b. A4e
   c. A Stake in the Outcome
   d. Advertising

8. _____ is a worldwide management consulting firm that focuses on solving issues of concern to senior management. McKinsey serves as an advisor to the world's leading businesses, governments, and institutions. It is widely recognized as a leader and one of the most prestigious firms in the management consulting industry.

   a. 33 Strategies of War
   b. 1990 Clean Air Act
   c. McKinsey ' Company
   d. 28-hour day

9. _____ is the term used to describe a situation where different entities cooperate advantageously for a final outcome. Simply defined, it means that the whole is greater than the sum of the individual parts. Although the whole will be greater than each individual part, this is not the concept of _____.

   a. 28-hour day
   b. 1990 Clean Air Act
   c. 33 Strategies of War
   d. Synergy

10. _____, or Value optimized pricing is a business strategy. It sets selling prices on the perceived value to the customer, rather than on the actual cost of the product, the market price, competitors prices, or the historical price.

    The goal of value-based pricing is to align price with value delivered.

    a. Centralization
    b. Chief legal officer
    c. Supervisory board
    d. Value based pricing

11. _____ is a term used in business to indicate a state of intense competitive rivalry accompanied by a multi-lateral series of price reduction. One competitor will lower its price, then others will lower their prices to match. If one of them reduces their price again, a new round of reductions starts.

    a. Pricing
    b. Price floor
    c. Price war
    d. Price ceiling

12. _____, in strategic management and marketing is, according to Carlton O'Neal, the percentage or proportion of the total available market or market segment that is being serviced by a company. It can be expressed as a company's sales revenue (from that market) divided by the total sales revenue available in that market. It can also be expressed as a company's unit sales volume (in a market) divided by the total volume of units sold in that market.

    a. Business-to-business
    b. Market share
    c. Marketing plan
    d. Green marketing

13. _____ is the pricing technique of setting a relatively low initial entry price, often lower than the eventual market price, to attract new customers. The strategy works on the expectation that customers will switch to the new brand because of the lower price. _____ is most commonly associated with a marketing objective of increasing market share or sales volume, rather than to make profit in the short term.

Chapter 11. Pricing and Credit Strategies

a. Penetration pricing
b. Transfer pricing
c. Pricing objectives
d. Price war

14. Why do retail stores need _____? With respect to the key objectives of growth and profit for any retail entity, _____ should significantly improve sales margins and increase sales by enabling the vendor to price variably and hence suitably and to control its product range based on profit margins. The retail stores will be able to compete more effectively with rivals in the form of mixed multiples, mail order and online retailers, who are often able to undercut but who do not generally have the same understanding of the retail market. In particular _____ is recognised as encouraging impulse buys, cross-selling of products and repeat sales.

a. 28-hour day
b. 33 Strategies of War
c. 1990 Clean Air Act
d. Dynamic pricing

15. _____ is an advertisement in which a particular product specifically mentions a competitor by name for the express purpose of showing why the competitor is inferior to the product naming it.

This should not be confused with parody advertisements, where a fictional product is being advertised for the purpose of poking fun at the particular advertisement, nor should it be confused with the use of a coined brand name for the purpose of comparing the product without actually naming an actual competitor. ('Wikipedia tastes better and is less filling than the Encyclopedia Galactica.')

In the 1980s, during what has been referred to as the cola wars, soft-drink manufacturer Pepsi ran a series of advertisements where people, caught on hidden camera, in a blind taste test, chose Pepsi over rival Coca-Cola.

a. 33 Strategies of War
b. 1990 Clean Air Act
c. 28-hour day
d. Comparative advertising

16. _____ is an unconventional system of promotions that relies on time, energy and imagination rather than a big marketing budget. Typically, _____ tactics are unexpected and unconventional; consumers are targeted in unexpected places, which can make the idea that's being marketed memorable, generate buzz, and even spread virally. The term was coined and defined by Jay Conrad Levinson in his 1984 book _____.

a. 28-hour day
b. Relationship marketing
c. 1990 Clean Air Act
d. Guerrilla marketing

17. _____ is an integrated communications-based process through which individuals and communities discover that existing and newly-identified needs and wants may be satisfied by the products and services of others.

_____ is defined by the American _____ Association as the activity, set of institutions, and processes for creating, communicating, delivering, and exchanging offerings that have value for customers, clients, partners, and society at large. The term developed from the original meaning which referred literally to going to market, as in shopping, or going to a market to buy or sell goods or services.

a. Market development
b. Disruptive technology
c. Customer relationship management
d. Marketing

18. A _____ is a secondary or incidental product deriving from a manufacturing process, a chemical reaction or a biochemical pathway, and is not the primary product or service being produced. A _____ can be useful and marketable, or it can be considered waste.

- dried blood and blood meal - from slaughterhouse operations
- chicken _____ meal - clean parts of the carcass of slaughtered chicken, such as necks, feet, undeveloped eggs, and intestines.
- chrome shavings - from a stage of leather manufacture
- collagen and gelatin - from the boiled skin and other parts of slaughtered livestock
- feathers - from poultry processing
    - feather meal - from poultry processing
- lanolin - from the cleaning of wool
- manure - from animal husbandry
- meat and bone meal - from the rendering of animal bones and offal
- poultry byproduct and poultry meal - made from unmarketable poultry bones and offal
- poultry litter - swept from the floors of chicken coops
- whey - from cheese manufacturing
- fetal pigs

- acidulated soap stock - from the refining of vegetable oil
- bran and germ - from the milling of whole grains into refined grains
- brewer's yeast - from ethanol fermentation
- cereal food fines - from breakfast cereal processing
- corn stover - residual plant matter after harvesting of cereals
- distillers grains - from ethanol fermentation
- glycerol - from the production of biodiesel
- grape seed oil - recovered from leftovers of the winemaking process
- molasses - from sugar refining
- orange oil and other citrus oils - recovered from the peels of processed fruit
- pectin - recovered from the remains of processed fruit
- sawdust and bark- from the processing of logs into lumber
- soybean meal - from soybean processing
- straw- from grain harvesting

- asphalt - from the refining of crude oil
- fly ash - from the combustion of coal
- slag - from ore refining
- gypsum - from Flue gas desulfurization
- ash and smoke - from the combustion of fuel
- mineral oil - from refining crude oil to produce gasoline
- salt - from desalination

- sludge - from wastewater treatment

Chapter 11. Pricing and Credit Strategies

a. By-product
c. Homeworkers
b. Manufacturing resource planning
d. Jidoka

19. The _____ requires the Federal government to investigate and pursue trusts, companies and organizations suspected of violating the Act. It was the first United States Federal statute to limit cartels and monopolies, and today still forms the basis for most antitrust litigation by the federal government.
a. 28-hour day
c. 33 Strategies of War
b. 1990 Clean Air Act
d. Sherman Antitrust Act

20. _____ is the difference between the cost of a good or service and its selling price. A _____ is added on to the total cost incurred by the producer of a good or service in order to create a profit. The total cost reflects the total amount of both fixed and variable expenses to produce and distribute a product.
a. Price points
c. Premium pricing
b. Markup
d. Topics

21. _____ is a pricing method used by companies. It is used primarily because it is easy to calculate and requires little information. There are several varieties, but the common thread in all of them is that one first calculates the cost of the product, then includes an additional amount to represent profit.
a. Target costing
c. Price discrimination
b. Cost-plus pricing
d. Price ceiling

22. Total _____ is a method of Accounting cost which entails the full cost of manufacturing or providing a service. This includes not just the costs of materials and labour, but also of all manufacturing overheads (whether 'fixed' or 'variable'.) One of the main reasons for absorbing overheads into the cost of units is for inventory valuation purposes.
a. A Stake in the Outcome
c. Absorption costing
b. AAAI
d. A4e

23. In cost-volume-profit analysis, a form of management accounting, _____ is the marginal profit per unit sale. It is a useful quantity in carrying out various calculations, and can be used as a measure of operating leverage.

The Total _____ is Total Revenue (TR, or Sales) minus Total Variable Cost (TVC):

TContribution margin = TR − TVC

The Unit _____ (C) is Unit Revenue (Price, P) minus Unit Variable Cost (V):

C = P − V

The _____ Ratio is the percentage of Contribution over Total Revenue, which can be calculated from the unit contribution over unit price or total contribution over Total Revenue:

$$\frac{C}{P} = \frac{P-V}{P} = \frac{\text{Unit Contribution Margin}}{\text{Price}} = \frac{\text{Total Contribution Margin}}{\text{Total Revenue}}$$

For instance, if the price is $10 and the unit variable cost is $2, then the unit _____ is $8, and the _____ ratio is $8/$10 = 80%.

a. Customer profitability
b. Factory overhead
c. Profit center
d. Contribution margin

24. _____ is a company's financial statement that indicates how the revenue is transformed into the net income The purpose of the _____ is to show managers and investors whether the company made or lost money during the period being reported.

The important thing to remember about an _____ is that it represents a period of time.

a. AAAI
b. Income statement
c. A Stake in the Outcome
d. A4e

25. _____, commonly known as e-commerce, consists of the buying and selling of products or services over electronic systems such as the Internet and other computer networks. The amount of trade conducted electronically has grown extraordinarily with widespread Internet usage. The use of commerce is conducted in this way, spurring and drawing on innovations in electronic funds transfer, supply chain management, Internet marketing, online transaction processing, electronic data interchange (EDI), inventory management systems, and automated data collection systems.

a. Online shopping
b. A Stake in the Outcome
c. A4e
d. Electronic Commerce

26. In the English-speaking world, a _____ , also called a Member Service Provider is an outside company that is contracted by a member bank to procure new merchant relationships for the specific bank.

a. AAAI
b. A4e
c. A Stake in the Outcome
d. Independent sales organization

27. _____ is a broad label that refers to any individuals or households that use goods and services generated within the economy. The concept of a _____ is used in different contexts, so that the usage and significance of the term may vary.

Typically when business people and economists talk of _____s they are talking about person as _____, an aggregated commodity item with little individuality other than that expressed in the buy/not-buy decision.

a. Consumer
b. 33 Strategies of War
c. 1990 Clean Air Act
d. 28-hour day

28. _____ exists when one firm provides goods or services to a customer with an agreement to bill them later, or receive a shipment or service from a supplier under an agreement to pay them later. It can be viewed as an essential element of capitalization in an operating business because it can reduce the required capital investment to operate the business if it is managed properly. _____ is the largest use of capital for a majority of business to business (B2B) sellers in the United States and is a critical source of capital for a majority of all businesses.

a. Countertrade
c. Buy-sell agreement
b. 1990 Clean Air Act
d. Trade credit

Chapter 12. Global Marketing Strategies

1. _____ is an integrated communications-based process through which individuals and communities discover that existing and newly-identified needs and wants may be satisfied by the products and services of others.

_____ is defined by the American _____ Association as the activity, set of institutions, and processes for creating, communicating, delivering, and exchanging offerings that have value for customers, clients, partners, and society at large. The term developed from the original meaning which referred literally to going to market, as in shopping, or going to a market to buy or sell goods or services.

   a. Disruptive technology
   b. Marketing
   c. Customer relationship management
   d. Market development

2. _____ is a worldwide management consulting firm that focuses on solving issues of concern to senior management. McKinsey serves as an advisor to the world's leading businesses, governments, and institutions. It is widely recognized as a leader and one of the most prestigious firms in the management consulting industry.
   a. 33 Strategies of War
   b. 28-hour day
   c. 1990 Clean Air Act
   d. McKinsey ' Company

3. _____ is the process of disassembly and recovery at the module level and, eventually, at the component level. It requires the repair or replacement of worn out or obsolete components and modules. Parts subject to degradation affecting the performance or the expected life of the whole are replaced.
   a. Remanufacturing
   b. Productivity
   c. Capacity planning
   d. Methods-time measurement

4. In economics, business, retail, and accounting, a _____ is the value of money that has been used up to produce something, and hence is not available for use anymore. In economics, a _____ is an alternative that is given up as a result of a decision. In business, the _____ may be one of acquisition, in which case the amount of money expended to acquire it is counted as _____.
   a. Fixed costs
   b. Cost allocation
   c. Cost overrun
   d. Cost

5. _____ Management is the succession of strategies used by management as a product goes through its _____. The conditions in which a product is sold changes over time and must be managed as it moves through its succession of stages.

The _____ goes through many phases, involves many professional disciplines, and requires many skills, tools and processes.

   a. Job hunting
   b. Golden handshake
   c. Strategic Alliance
   d. Product life cycle

6. _____ is a form of communication that typically attempts to persuade potential customers to purchase or to consume more of a particular brand of product or service. 'While now central to the contemporary global economy and the reproduction of global production networks, it is only quite recently that _____ has been more than a marginal influence on patterns of sales and production. The formation of modern _____ was intimately bound up with the emergence of new forms of monopoly capitalism around the end of the 19th and beginning of the 20th century as one element in corporate strategies to create, organize and where possible control markets, especially for mass produced consumer goods.

Chapter 12. Global Marketing Strategies

a. AAAI
b. A Stake in the Outcome
c. A4e
d. Advertising

7. A _____ is a business that is privately owned and operated, with a small number of employees and relatively low volume of sales. The legal definition of 'small' often varies by country and industry, but is generally under 100 employees in the United States and under 50 employees in the European Union. In comparison, the definition of mid-sized business by the number of employees is generally under 500 in the U.S. and 250 for the European Union.

a. Golden Boot Compensation
b. Small business
c. Pre-determined overhead rate
d. Critical Success Factor

8. _____ is exchange of capital, goods, and services across international borders or territories. In most countries, it represents a significant share of gross domestic product (GDP.) While _____ has been present throughout much of history, its economic, social, and political importance has been on the rise in recent centuries.

a. A4e
b. AAAI
c. A Stake in the Outcome
d. International Trade

9. Marketing research is a form of business research and is generally divided into two categories: consumer _____ and business-to-business (B2B) _____, which was previously known as industrial marketing research. Consumer marketing research studies the buying habits of individual people while business-to-business marketing research investigates the markets for products sold by one business to another.

Consumer _____ is a form of applied sociology that concentrates on understanding the behaviours, whims and preferences, of consumers in a market-based economy, and aims to understand the effects and comparative success of marketing campaigns.

a. Market research
b. Questionnaire
c. Mystery shoppers
d. Questionnaire construction

10. An _____ is an organization founded and funded by businesses that operate in a specific industry. An industry trade association participates in public relations activities such as advertising, education, political donations, lobbying and publishing, but its main focus is collaboration between companies, or standardization. Associations may offer other services, such as producing conferences, networking or charitable events or offering classes or educational materials.

a. Industry trade group
b. A Stake in the Outcome
c. A4e
d. AAAI

11. The 'business case for _____', theorizes that in a global marketplace, a company that employs a diverse workforce (both men and women, people of many generations, people from ethnically and racially diverse backgrounds etc.) is better able to understand the demographics of the marketplace it serves and is thus better equipped to thrive in that marketplace than a company that has a more limited range of employee demographics.

An additional corollary suggests that a company that supports the _____ of its workforce can also improve employee satisfaction, productivity and retention.

a. Kanban
b. Virtual team
c. Trademark
d. Diversity

Chapter 12. Global Marketing Strategies

12. _____ is an advertisement in which a particular product specifically mentions a competitor by name for the express purpose of showing why the competitor is inferior to the product naming it.

This should not be confused with parody advertisements, where a fictional product is being advertised for the purpose of poking fun at the particular advertisement, nor should it be confused with the use of a coined brand name for the purpose of comparing the product without actually naming an actual competitor. ('Wikipedia tastes better and is less filling than the Encyclopedia Galactica.')

In the 1980s, during what has been referred to as the cola wars, soft-drink manufacturer Pepsi ran a series of advertisements where people, caught on hidden camera, in a blind taste test, chose Pepsi over rival Coca-Cola.

a. 33 Strategies of War
b. 28-hour day
c. 1990 Clean Air Act
d. Comparative advertising

13. The _____ is a United States government agency that provides support to small businesses.

The mission of the _____ is 'to maintain and strengthen the nation's economy by enabling the establishment and viability of small businesses and by assisting in the economic recovery of communities after disasters.'

The _____ makes loans directly to businesses and acts as a guarantor on bank loans. In some circumstances it also makes loans to victims of natural disasters, works to get government procurement contracts for small businesses, and assists businesses with management, technical and training issues.

a. 1990 Clean Air Act
b. Small Business Administration
c. 28-hour day
d. 33 Strategies of War

14. A _____ is an entity formed between two or more parties to undertake economic activity together. The parties agree to create a new entity by both contributing equity, and they then share in the revenues, expenses, and control of the enterprise. The venture can be for one specific project only, or a continuing business relationship such as the Fuji Xerox _____.

a. Patent
b. Civil Rights Act of 1991
c. Meritor Savings Bank v. Vinson
d. Joint venture

15. The _____ is the Cabinet department of the United States government concerned with promoting economic growth. It was originally created as the _____ and Labor on February 14, 1903. It was subsequently renamed to the Department of Commerce on March 4, 1913, and its bureaus and agencies specializing in labor were transferred to the new Department of Labor.

a. AAAI
b. United States Department of Commerce
c. A4e
d. A Stake in the Outcome

16. An _____ is a person who has possession of an enterprise and assumes significant accountability for the inherent risks and the outcome. It is an ambitious leader who combines land, labor, and capital to create and market new goods or services. The term is a loanword from French and was first defined by the Irish economist Richard Cantillon.

a. AAAI
b. A4e
c. A Stake in the Outcome
d. Entrepreneur

Chapter 12. Global Marketing Strategies

17. _____ refers to the methods of practicing and using another person's business philosophy. The franchisor grants the independent operator the right to distribute its products, techniques, and trademarks for a percentage of gross monthly sales and a royalty fee. Various tangibles and intangibles such as national or international advertising, training, and other support services are commonly made available by the franchisor.

a. Franchising
b. ServiceMaster
c. 28-hour day
d. 1990 Clean Air Act

18. _____ is one of the four elements of marketing mix. An organization or set of organizations (go-betweens) involved in the process of making a product or service available for use or consumption by a consumer or business user.

The other three parts of the marketing mix are product, pricing, and promotion.

a. Matching theory
b. Missing completely at random
c. Job creation programs
d. Distribution

19. A _____ is a documented investigation of a Market that is used to inform a firm's planning activities particularly around decision of: inventory, purchase, work force expansion/contraction, facility expansion, purchases of capital equipment, promotional activities, and many other aspects of a company.

Not all managers are asked to conduct a _____, but all managers must make decisions using _____ data and understand how the data was derived. So all managers need a reasonable understanding of the tools most used for making sales forecasts and analyzing markets.

a. Marketing research process
b. 1990 Clean Air Act
c. Market Analysis
d. Marketing research

20. The _____ of 1977 (15 U.S.C. §§ 78dd-1, et seq.) is a United States federal law known primarily for two of its main provisions, one that addresses accounting transparency requirements under the Securities Exchange Act of 1934 and another concerning bribery of foreign officials.

a. Social Security Act of 1965
b. Meritor Savings Bank v. Vinson
c. Limited liability
d. Foreign Corrupt Practices Act

21. A standard, commercial _____ is a document issued mostly by a financial institution, used primarily in trade finance, which usually provides an irrevocable payment undertaking.

The LC can also be the source of payment for a traction, meaning that redeeming the _____ will pay an exporter. Letters of credit are used primarily in international trade transactions of significant value, for deals between a supplier in one country and a customer in another.

a. Sarbanes-Oxley Act of 2002
b. Letter of credit
c. False Claims Act
d. Diminishing returns

22. A _____ is a relatively new executive level position at a corporation, company, organization typically reporting directly to the CEO or board of directors. The _____ is responsible for a brand's image, experience, and promise, and propagating it throughout all aspects of the company. The brand officer oversees marketing, advertising, design, public relations and customer service departments.

Chapter 12. Global Marketing Strategies

a. Chief executive officer
b. Purchasing manager
c. Director of communications
d. Chief brand officer

23. _____ is subcontracting a process, such as product design or manufacturing, to a third-party company. The decision to outsource is often made in the interest of lowering cost or making better use of time and energy costs, redirecting or conserving energy directed at the competencies of a particular business, or to make more efficient use of land, labor, capital, (information) technology and resources. _____ became part of the business lexicon during the 1980s.
   a. Operant conditioning
   b. Outsourcing
   c. Unemployment insurance
   d. Opinion leadership

24. _____ are legal property rights over creations of the mind, both artistic and commercial, and the corresponding fields of law. Under _____ law, owners are granted certain exclusive rights to a variety of intangible assets, such as musical, literary, and artistic works; ideas, discoveries and inventions; and words, phrases, symbols, and designs. Common types of _____ include copyrights, trademarks, patents, industrial design rights and trade secrets.
   a. Unemployment Action Center
   b. Intellectual property
   c. Equal Pay Act
   d. Intent

25. _____ plant, and equipment, is a term used in accountancy for assets and property which cannot easily be converted into cash. This can be compared with current assets such as cash or bank accounts, which are described as liquid assets. In most cases, only tangible assets are referred to as fixed.
   a. 33 Strategies of War
   b. 1990 Clean Air Act
   c. 28-hour day
   d. Fixed asset

26. A _____ is a general term that describes any government policy or regulation that restricts international trade. The barriers can take many forms, including the following terms that include many restrictions in international trade within multiple countries that import and export any items of trade.

- Import duty
- Import licenses
- Export licenses
- Import quotas
- Tariffs
- Subsidies
- Non-tariff barriers to trade
- Voluntary Export Restraints
- Local Content Requirements
- Embargo

Most _____s work on the same principle: the imposition of some sort of cost on trade that raises the price of the traded products. If two or more nations repeatedly use _____s against each other, then a trade war results.

a. Most favoured nation
b. Customs brokerage
c. Trade barrier
d. Trade creation

Chapter 12. Global Marketing Strategies

27. The _____ was the outcome of the failure of negotiating governments to create the International Trade Organization (ITO.) GATT was formed in 1947 and lasted until 1994, when it was replaced by the World Trade Organization. The Bretton Woods Conference had introduced the idea for an organization to regulate trade as part of a larger plan for economic recovery after World War II.
   a. Multilateral treaty
   b. 28-hour day
   c. 1990 Clean Air Act
   d. General Agreement on Tariffs and Trade

28. The _____ is an international organization designed by its founders to supervise and liberalize international trade. The organization officially commenced on 1 January 1995, under the Marrakesh Agreement, succeeding the 1947 General Agreement on Tariffs and Trade (GATT.)

The _____ deals with regulation of trade between participating countries; it provides a framework for negotiating and formalising trade agreements, and a dispute resolution process aimed at enforcing participants' adherence to _____ agreements which are signed by representatives of member governments and ratified by their parliaments.

   a. 1990 Clean Air Act
   b. National Institute for Occupational Safety and Health
   c. Network planning and design
   d. World Trade Organization

29. _____ is a type of trade policy that allows traders to act and transact without interference from government. Thus, the policy permits trading partners mutual gains from trade, with goods and services produced according to the theory of comparative advantage.

Under a _____ policy, prices are a reflection of true supply and demand, and are the sole determinant of resource allocation.

   a. 1990 Clean Air Act
   b. 28-hour day
   c. Free trade
   d. 33 Strategies of War

30. The _____ is a treaty of the World Trade Organization (WTO) that entered into force in January 1995 as a result of the Uruguay Round negotiations. The treaty was created to extend the multilateral trading system to service sector, in the same way the General Agreement on Tariffs and Trade (GATT) provides such a system for merchandise trade.
   a. 28-hour day
   b. General Agreement on Trade in Services
   c. 33 Strategies of War
   d. 1990 Clean Air Act

Chapter 13. E-Commerce and Entrepreneurship

1. _____ was a writer, management consultant, and self-described 'social ecologist.' Widely considered to be 'the father of modern management,' his 39 books and countless scholarly and popular articles explored how humans are organized across all sectors of society--in business, government and the nonprofit world. His writings have predicted many of the major developments of the late twentieth century, including privatization and decentralization; the rise of Japan to economic world power; the decisive importance of marketing; and the emergence of the information society with its necessity of lifelong learning. In 1959, Drucker coined the term 'knowledge worker' and later in his life considered knowledge work productivity to be the next frontier of management.

   a. Debora L. Spar
   b. Peter Ferdinand Drucker
   c. Jacques Al-Salawat Nasruddin Nasser
   d. Chrissie Hynde

2. _____, commonly known as e-commerce, consists of the buying and selling of products or services over electronic systems such as the Internet and other computer networks. The amount of trade conducted electronically has grown extraordinarily with widespread Internet usage. The use of commerce is conducted in this way, spurring and drawing on innovations in electronic funds transfer, supply chain management, Internet marketing, online transaction processing, electronic data interchange (EDI), inventory management systems, and automated data collection systems.

   a. Online shopping
   b. A Stake in the Outcome
   c. A4e
   d. Electronic Commerce

3. _____ is the provision of service to customers before, during and after a purchase.

   According to Turban et al. (2002), '_____ is a series of activities designed to enhance the level of customer satisfaction - that is, the feeling that a product or service has met the customer expectation.'

   Its importance varies by product, industry and customer; defective or broken merchandise can be exchanged, often only with a receipt and within a specified time frame.

   a. Service rate
   b. 28-hour day
   c. 1990 Clean Air Act
   d. Customer service

4. _____ is an integrated communications-based process through which individuals and communities discover that existing and newly-identified needs and wants may be satisfied by the products and services of others.

   _____ is defined by the American _____ Association as the activity, set of institutions, and processes for creating, communicating, delivering, and exchanging offerings that have value for customers, clients, partners, and society at large. The term developed from the original meaning which referred literally to going to market, as in shopping, or going to a market to buy or sell goods or services.

   a. Disruptive technology
   b. Customer relationship management
   c. Market development
   d. Marketing

5. _____ is an advertisement in which a particular product specifically mentions a competitor by name for the express purpose of showing why the competitor is inferior to the product naming it.

   This should not be confused with parody advertisements, where a fictional product is being advertised for the purpose of poking fun at the particular advertisement, nor should it be confused with the use of a coined brand name for the purpose of comparing the product without actually naming an actual competitor. ('Wikipedia tastes better and is less filling than the Encyclopedia Galactica.')

Chapter 13. E-Commerce and Entrepreneurship

In the 1980s, during what has been referred to as the cola wars, soft-drink manufacturer Pepsi ran a series of advertisements where people, caught on hidden camera, in a blind taste test, chose Pepsi over rival Coca-Cola.

a. 33 Strategies of War
c. 28-hour day

b. 1990 Clean Air Act
d. Comparative advertising

6. In economics, business, retail, and accounting, a _____ is the value of money that has been used up to produce something, and hence is not available for use anymore. In economics, a _____ is an alternative that is given up as a result of a decision. In business, the _____ may be one of acquisition, in which case the amount of money expended to acquire it is counted as _____.

a. Fixed costs
c. Cost overrun

b. Cost allocation
d. Cost

7. _____ is a term used to describe the demographic cohort following Generation X. Its members are often referred to as 'Millennials' or 'Echo Boomers') . There are no precise dates for when Gen Y begins and ends. Most commentators use dates from the early 1980s to early 1990s.

a. Giovanni Agnelli
c. David Wittig

b. Generation Y
d. Benjamin R. Barber

8.

The _____ can vary from one organization to another but there are some key elements that are common throughout

The process usually starts with a 'Demand' or requirements - this could be for a physical part (inventory) or a service. A requisition is generated, which details the requirements (in some cases providing a requirements speciation) which actions the procurement department. An RFP or RFQ is then raised (request for proposal or Request for quotation.)

a. Request for quotation
c. Purchase requisition

b. 1990 Clean Air Act
d. Purchasing process

9. _____ is a form of communication that typically attempts to persuade potential customers to purchase or to consume more of a particular brand of product or service. 'While now central to the contemporary global economy and the reproduction of global production networks, it is only quite recently that _____ has been more than a marginal influence on patterns of sales and production. The formation of modern _____ was intimately bound up with the emergence of new forms of monopoly capitalism around the end of the 19th and beginning of the 20th century as one element in corporate strategies to create, organize and where possible control markets, especially for mass produced consumer goods.

a. Advertising
c. A4e

b. AAAI
d. A Stake in the Outcome

Chapter 13. E-Commerce and Entrepreneurship

10. _____ refers to the movement of cash into or out of a business or financial product. It is usually measured during a specified, finite period of time. Measurement of _____ can be used

- to determine a project's rate of return or value. The time of _____s into and out of projects are used as inputs in financial models such as internal rate of return, and net present value.
- to determine problems with a business's liquidity. Being profitable does not necessarily mean being liquid. A company can fail because of a shortage of cash, even while profitable.
- as an alternate measure of a business's profits when it is believed that accrual accounting concepts do not represent economic realities. For example, a company may be notionally profitable but generating little operational cash (as may be the case for a company that barters its products rather than selling for cash.) In such a case, the company may be deriving additional operating cash by issuing shares evaluating default risk, re-investment requirements, etc.

_____ is a generic term used differently depending on the context. It may be defined by users for their own purposes.

a. Gross profit
c. Sweat equity
b. Gross profit margin
d. Cash flow

11. A _____ is a name or trademark connected with a product or producer. _____s have become increasingly important components of culture and the economy, now being described as 'cultural accessories and personal philosophies'.

Some people distinguish the psychological aspect of a _____ from the experiential aspect.

a. Brand awareness
c. Brand loyalty
b. Brand extension
d. Brand

12. A _____ is a business that is privately owned and operated, with a small number of employees and relatively low volume of sales. The legal definition of 'small' often varies by country and industry, but is generally under 100 employees in the United States and under 50 employees in the European Union. In comparison, the definition of mid-sized business by the number of employees is generally under 500 in the U.S. and 250 for the European Union.

a. Golden Boot Compensation
c. Critical Success Factor
b. Pre-determined overhead rate
d. Small Business

13. In decision theory and estimation theory, the _____ of an estimator, $\hat{\theta}$, of an unknown parameter of the distribution, θ, is the expected value of the loss function

$$R(\theta, \hat{\theta}) = \mathbb{E}_\theta L(\theta, \hat{\theta}) = \int L(\theta, \hat{\theta}) \, dP_\theta.$$

Chapter 13. E-Commerce and Entrepreneurship

where dP_θ is a probability measure parametrized by θ.

- For a scalar parameter θ and a quadratic loss function,

$$L(\theta, \hat{\theta}) = (\theta - \hat{\theta})^2$$

the _____ function becomes the mean squared error of the estimate,

$$R(\theta, \hat{\theta}) = E_\theta (\theta - \hat{\theta})^2$$

- In density estimation, the unknown parameter is probability density itself. The loss function is typically chosen to be a norm in an appropriate function space. For example, for L^2 norm,

$$L(f, \hat{f}) = \|f - \hat{f}\|_2^2$$

the _____ function becomes the mean integrated squared error

$$R(f, \hat{f}) = E\|f - \hat{f}\|^2$$

a. Financial modeling
c. Linear model
b. Risk aversion
d. Risk

14. _____ describes commerce transactions between businesses, such as between a manufacturer and a wholesaler, or between a wholesaler and a retailer. Contrasting terms are business-to-consumer (B2C) and business-to-government (B2G.)

The volume of B2B transactions is much higher than the volume of B2C transactions.

a. Market environment
c. Product bundling
b. Category management
d. Business-to-business

15. _____ or promotional products refers to articles of merchandise that are used in marketing and communication programs. These items are usually imprinted with a company's name, logo or slogan, and given away at trade shows, conferences, and as part of guerrilla marketing campaigns.

Almost anything can be branded with a company's name or logo and used for promotion.

a. 1990 Clean Air Act
c. 28-hour day
b. 33 Strategies of War
d. Promotional items

Chapter 13. E-Commerce and Entrepreneurship

16. _____ is the practice of managing the flow of information between an organization and its publics. _____ gains an organization or individual exposure to their audiences using topics of public interest and news items that do not require direct payment. Because _____ places exposure in credible third-party outlets, it offers a third-party legitimacy that advertising does not have.

   a. 1990 Clean Air Act
   b. Public Relations
   c. 28-hour day
   d. Two-way communication

17. A _____ is a formal relationship between two or more parties to pursue a set of agreed upon goals or to meet a critical business need while remaining independent organizations.

Partners may provide the _____ with resources such as products, distribution channels, manufacturing capability, project funding, capital equipment, knowledge, expertise, or intellectual property. The alliance is a cooperation or collaboration which aims for a synergy where each partner hopes that the benefits from the alliance will be greater than those from individual efforts.

   a. Process automation
   b. Strategic alliance
   c. Golden parachute
   d. Farmshoring

18. The loyalty business model is a business model used in strategic management in which company resources are employed so as to increase the loyalty of customers and other stakeholders in the expectation that corporate objectives will be met or surpassed. A typical example of this type of model is: quality of product or service leads to customer satisfaction, which leads to _____, which leads to profitability.

Fredrick Reichheld (1996) expanded the loyalty business model beyond customers and employees.

   a. Customer loyalty
   b. 1990 Clean Air Act
   c. 28-hour day
   d. 33 Strategies of War

19. A _____ is a set of exclusive rights granted by a state to an inventor or his assignee for a limited period of time in exchange for a disclosure of an invention.

The procedure for granting _____s, the requirements placed on the _____ee and the extent of the exclusive rights vary widely between countries according to national laws and international agreements. Typically, however, a _____ application must include one or more claims defining the invention which must be new, inventive, and useful or industrially applicable.

   a. Labor Management Reporting and Disclosure Act
   b. Federal Trade Commission Act
   c. Food, Drug, and Cosmetic Act
   d. Patent

20. A _____ is a distinctive sign or indicator used by an individual, business organization, or other legal entity to identify that the products and/or services to consumers with which the _____ appears originate from a unique source and to distinguish its products or services from those of other entities.

   a. Kanban
   b. Succession planning
   c. Virtual team
   d. Trademark

21. _____ is 'the action or practice of selling among or between established clients, markets, traders, etc.' or 'that of selling an additional product or service to an existing customer'. In practice businesses define _____ in many different ways. Elements that might influence the definition might include: the size of the business, the industry sector it operates within and the financial motivations of those required to define the term. The objectives of _____ can be either to increase the income derived from the client or to protect the relationship with the client(s).

a. Business networking
c. Gap analysis
b. Yield management
d. Cross-selling

22. _____ is the measurement, collection, analysis and reporting of internet data for purposes of understanding and optimizing web usage.

There are two categories of _____; off-site and on-site _____.

Off-site _____ refers to web measurement and analysis irrespective of whether you own or maintain a website. On-site _____ measure a visitor's journey once on your website.

a. 33 Strategies of War
c. 1990 Clean Air Act
b. 28-hour day
d. Web analytics

23. The phrase mergers and _____s refers to the aspect of corporate strategy, corporate finance and management dealing with the buying, selling and combining of different companies that can aid, finance, or help a growing company in a given industry grow rapidly without having to create another business entity.

An _____, also known as a takeover or a buyout, is the buying of one company (the 'target') by another. An _____ may be friendly or hostile.

a. AAAI
c. A Stake in the Outcome
b. A4e
d. Acquisition

24. _____ is the intelligence of machines and the branch of computer science which aims to create it. Major _____ textbooks define the field as 'the study and design of intelligent agents,' where an intelligent agent is a system that perceives its environment and takes actions which maximize its chances of success. John McCarthy, who coined the term in 1956, defines it as 'the science and engineering of making intelligent machines.'

The field was founded on the claim that a central property of human beings, intelligence--the sapience of Homo sapiens--can be so precisely described that it can be simulated by a machine.

a. AAAI
c. A Stake in the Outcome
b. A4e
d. Artificial intelligence

25. _____ is the process of filtering for information or patterns using techniques involving collaboration among multiple agents, viewpoints, data sources, etc. Applications of _____ typically involve very large data sets. _____ methods have been applied to many different kinds of data including sensing and monitoring data - such as in mineral exploration, environmental sensing over large areas or multiple sensors; financial data - such as financial service institutions that integrate many financial sources; or in electronic commerce and web 2.0 applications where the focus is on user data, etc.

Chapter 13. E-Commerce and Entrepreneurship

    a. 33 Strategies of War
    c. Collaborative filtering
    b. 1990 Clean Air Act
    d. 28-hour day

26. A _____ is the return of funds to a consumer, forcibly initiated by the consumer's issuing bank. Specifically, it is the reversal of a prior outbound transfer of funds from a consumer's bank account or line of credit.

The _____ mechanism exists primarily for consumer protection.

    a. 1990 Clean Air Act
    c. 33 Strategies of War
    b. 28-hour day
    d. Chargeback

Chapter 14. Sources of Equity Financing

1. An _____ is any party that makes an investment.

The term has taken on a specific meaning in finance to describe the particular types of people and companies that regularly purchase equity or debt securities for financial gain in exchange for funding an expanding company. Less frequently, the term is applied to parties who purchase real estate, currency, commodity derivatives, personal property, or other assets.

a. A Stake in the Outcome
b. Investor
c. AAAI
d. A4e

2. _____ is a type of private equity investment, most often a minority investment, in relatively mature companies that are looking for capital to expand or restructure operations, enter new markets or finance a significant acquisition without a change of control of the business.

Companies that seek _____, will often do so in order to finance a transformational event in their lifecycle. These companies are likely to be more mature than venture capital funded companies, able to generate revenue and operating profits but unable to generate sufficient cash to fund major expansions, acquisitions or other investments.

a. Growth capital
b. Management buyout
c. Seed round
d. Pension fund

3. _____ is a financial metric which represents operating liquidity available to a business. Along with fixed assets such as plant and equipment, _____ is considered a part of operating capital. It is calculated as current assets minus current liabilities.

a. 33 Strategies of War
b. 28-hour day
c. Working capital
d. 1990 Clean Air Act

4. A _____ is a formal statement of a set of business goals, the reasons why they are believed attainable, and the plan for reaching those goals. It may also contain background information about the organization or team attempting to reach those goals.

The business goals may be defined for for-profit or for non-profit organizations.

a. Business plan
b. Time management
c. Distributed management
d. Crisis management

5. _____ according to Onuoha (2007) is the practice of starting new organizations or revitalizing mature organizations, particularly new businesses generally in response to identified opportunities. _____ is often a difficult undertaking, as a vast majority of new businesses fail. Entrepreneurial activities are substantially different depending on the type of organization that is being started.

a. AAAI
b. A4e
c. A Stake in the Outcome
d. Entrepreneurship

6. _____ is a civil designation for persons who are incorporated in a fixed or permanent way to a society or group: regular member of the working staff, permanent staff distinguished from a supernumerary.

Chapter 14. Sources of Equity Financing

The term '_____' and its counterpart, 'supernumerary,' originated in Spanish and Latin American academy and government; it is now also used in countries all over the world, such as France, the U.S., England, Italy, etc.

There are _____ members of surgical organizations, of universities, of gastronomical associations, etc.

- a. Adam Smith
- b. Abraham Harold Maslow
- c. Affiliation
- d. Numerary

7. _____ is a lightweight markup language, originally created by John Gruber and Aaron Swartz to help maximum readability and 'publishability' of both its input and output forms. The language takes many cues from existing conventions for marking up plain text in email. _____ converts its marked-up text input to valid, well-formed XHTML and replaces left-pointing angle brackets ('<') and ampersands with their corresponding character entity references.
- a. 33 Strategies of War
- b. 1990 Clean Air Act
- c. Markdown
- d. 28-hour day

8. An _____ is a person who has possession of an enterprise and assumes significant accountability for the inherent risks and the outcome. It is an ambitious leader who combines land, labor, and capital to create and market new goods or services. The term is a loanword from French and was first defined by the Irish economist Richard Cantillon.
- a. A Stake in the Outcome
- b. A4e
- c. AAAI
- d. Entrepreneur

9. A _____ is a type of business entity in which partners (owners) share with each other the profits or losses of the business. _____s are often favored over corporations for taxation purposes, as the _____ structure does not generally incur a tax on profits before it is distributed to the partners (i.e. there is no dividend tax levied.) However, depending on the _____ structure and the jurisdiction in which it operates, owners of a _____ may be exposed to greater personal liability than they would as shareholders of a corporation.
- a. Mediation
- b. Partnership
- c. Due process
- d. Federal Employers Liability Act

10. A _____ is a business that is privately owned and operated, with a small number of employees and relatively low volume of sales. The legal definition of 'small' often varies by country and industry, but is generally under 100 employees in the United States and under 50 employees in the European Union. In comparison, the definition of mid-sized business by the number of employees is generally under 500 in the U.S. and 250 for the European Union.
- a. Critical Success Factor
- b. Pre-determined overhead rate
- c. Golden Boot Compensation
- d. Small Business

11. The _____ is a United States government agency that provides support to small businesses.

The mission of the _____ is 'to maintain and strengthen the nation's economy by enabling the establishment and viability of small businesses and by assisting in the economic recovery of communities after disasters.'

The _____ makes loans directly to businesses and acts as a guarantor on bank loans. In some circumstances it also makes loans to victims of natural disasters, works to get government procurement contracts for small businesses, and assists businesses with management, technical and training issues.

Chapter 14. Sources of Equity Financing

89

a. Small Business Administration
b. 33 Strategies of War
c. 1990 Clean Air Act
d. 28-hour day

12. _____ is a type of private equity capital typically provided to early-stage, high-potential, growth companies in the interest of generating a return through an eventual realization event such as an IPO or trade sale of the company. _____ investments are generally made as cash in exchange for shares in the invested company. It is typical for _____ investors to identify and back companies in high technology industries such as biotechnology and ICT.
   a. Seed round
   b. Private equity
   c. Limited liability corporation
   d. Venture capital

13. A _____ is a relatively new executive level position at a corporation, company, organization typically reporting directly to the CEO or board of directors. The _____ is responsible for a brand's image, experience, and promise, and propagating it throughout all aspects of the company. The brand officer oversees marketing, advertising, design, public relations and customer service departments.
   a. Chief executive officer
   b. Director of communications
   c. Purchasing manager
   d. Chief brand officer

14. _____ is the state or fact of exclusive rights and control over property, which may be an object, land/real estate or intellectual property. An _____ right is also referred to as title. The concept of _____ has existed for thousands of years and in all cultures.
   a. A Stake in the Outcome
   b. Ownership
   c. Emanation of the state
   d. A4e

15. _____ refers to the movement of cash into or out of a business or financial product. It is usually measured during a specified, finite period of time. Measurement of _____ can be used

   - to determine a project's rate of return or value. The time of _____s into and out of projects are used as inputs in financial models such as internal rate of return, and net present value.
   - to determine problems with a business's liquidity. Being profitable does not necessarily mean being liquid. A company can fail because of a shortage of cash, even while profitable.
   - as an alternate measure of a business's profits when it is believed that accrual accounting concepts do not represent economic realities. For example, a company may be notionally profitable but generating little operational cash (as may be the case for a company that barters its products rather than selling for cash.) In such a case, the company may be deriving additional operating cash by issuing shares evaluating default risk, re-investment requirements, etc.

   _____ is a generic term used differently depending on the context. It may be defined by users for their own purposes.

   a. Gross profit margin
   b. Sweat equity
   c. Gross profit
   d. Cash flow

16. _____ , also referred to simply as a 'public offering' or 'flotation,' is when a company issues common stock or shares to the public for the first time. They are often issued by smaller, younger companies seeking capital to expand, but can also be done by large privately-owned companies looking to become publicly traded.

Chapter 14. Sources of Equity Financing

In an _____ the issuer may obtain the assistance of an underwriting firm, which helps it determine what type of security to issue (common or preferred), best offering price and time to bring it to market.

a. Unemployment insurance
b. Occupational Safety and Health Administration
c. Outsourcing
d. Initial public offering

17. A _____ refers to how a corporation is perceived. It is a generally accepted image of what a company 'stands for'. The creation of a _____ is an exercise in perception management.
a. Marketing
b. Context analysis
c. Market development
d. Corporate image

18. The phrase mergers and _____s refers to the aspect of corporate strategy, corporate finance and management dealing with the buying, selling and combining of different companies that can aid, finance, or help a growing company in a given industry grow rapidly without having to create another business entity.

An _____, also known as a takeover or a buyout, is the buying of one company (the 'target') by another. An _____ may be friendly or hostile.

a. Acquisition
b. AAAI
c. A4e
d. A Stake in the Outcome

19. The National Association of Securities Dealers Automated Quotations known as _____, is an American stock exchange. It is the largest electronic screen-based equity securities trading market in the United States. With approximately 3,800 companies and corporations, it has more trading volume per hour than any other stock exchange in the world.
a. 28-hour day
b. 1990 Clean Air Act
c. 33 Strategies of War
d. NASDAQ

20. The _____ of 2002 (Pub.L. 107-204, 116 Stat. 745, enacted July 30, 2002), also known as the Public Company Accounting Reform and Investor Protection Act of 2002 and commonly called Sarbanes-Oxley, Sarbox or SOX, is a United States federal law enacted on July 30, 2002, as a reaction to a number of major corporate and accounting scandals including those affecting Enron, Tyco International, Adelphia, Peregrine Systems and WorldCom.
a. Sarbanes-Oxley Act of 2002
b. Fair Labor Standards Act
c. Letter of credit
d. Sarbanes-Oxley Act

21. The U.S. _____ is an independent agency of the United States government which holds primary responsibility for enforcing the federal securities laws and regulating the securities industry, the nation's stock and options exchanges, and other electronic securities markets. The SEC was created by section 4 of the Securities Exchange Act of 1934 (now codified as 15 U.S.C. § 78d and commonly referred to as the 1934 Act.)
a. 1990 Clean Air Act
b. 28-hour day
c. 33 Strategies of War
d. Securities and Exchange Commission

22. _____ is a concept in ethics with several meanings. It is often used synonymously with such concepts as responsibility, answerability, enforcement, blameworthiness, liability and other terms associated with the expectation of account-giving. As an aspect of governance, it has been central to discussions related to problems in both the public and private (corporation) worlds.

Chapter 14. Sources of Equity Financing

a. A4e
b. A Stake in the Outcome
c. Usury
d. Accountability

23. A mutual _____ or stockholder is an individual or company (including a corporation) that legally owns one or more shares of stock in a joint stock company. A company's _____s collectively own that company. Thus, the typical goal of such companies is to enhance _____ value.
a. Stockholder
b. Free riding
c. 1990 Clean Air Act
d. Shareholder

24. _____, commonly known as e-commerce, consists of the buying and selling of products or services over electronic systems such as the Internet and other computer networks. The amount of trade conducted electronically has grown extraordinarily with widespread Internet usage. The use of commerce is conducted in this way, spurring and drawing on innovations in electronic funds transfer, supply chain management, Internet marketing, online transaction processing, electronic data interchange (EDI), inventory management systems, and automated data collection systems.
a. Electronic Commerce
b. Online shopping
c. A4e
d. A Stake in the Outcome

25. A _____ is a process in which a potential employee is evaluated by an employer for prospective employment in their company, organization and was established in the late 16th century.

A _____ typically precedes the hiring decision, and is used to evaluate the candidate. The interview is usually preceded by the evaluation of submitted résumés from interested candidates, then selecting a small number of candidates for interviews.

a. Payrolling
b. Supported employment
c. Split shift
d. Job interview

26. _____ is a document outlining an agreement between two or more parties before the agreement is finalized. The concept is similar to the so-called heads of agreement. Such agreements may be Asset Purchase Agreements, Share Purchase Agreements, Joint-Venture Agreements and overall all Agreements which aim at closing a financially large deal.
a. 28-hour day
b. 1990 Clean Air Act
c. Letter of intent
d. 33 Strategies of War

27. Under the Securities Act of 1933, any offer to sell securities must either be registered with the SEC or meet an exemption. _____ contains three rules providing exemptions from the registration requirements, allowing some companies to offer and sell their securities without having to register the securities with the SEC. Rule 501 of Reg D contains definitions that apply to the rest of Reg D. Rule 502 contains the general conditions that must be met to take advantage of the exemptions under _____. Generally speaking, these conditions are (1) that all sales within a certain time period that are part of the same Reg D offering must be 'integrated', meaning they must be treated as one offering, (2) information and disclosures must be provided, (3) there must be no 'general solicitation', and (4) that the securities being sold contain restrictions on their resale.
a. 28-hour day
b. 33 Strategies of War
c. Regulation D
d. 1990 Clean Air Act

Chapter 14. Sources of Equity Financing

28. A _____ is a funding round of securities which are sold without a initial public offering, usually to a small number of chosen private investors. In the United States, these placements are not subject to the Securities Act of 1933 and do not have to be registered with the Securities and Exchange Commission, although the sale must conform to SEC rules. _____s may typically consist of stocks, shares or warrants and purchasers are often institutional investors such as banks, insurance companies or pension funds.

a. Labor intensive
b. Private Placement
c. Niche market
d. Choquet integral

Chapter 15. Sources of Debt Financing

1. _____, in strategic management and marketing is, according to Carlton O'Neal, the percentage or proportion of the total available market or market segment that is being serviced by a company. It can be expressed as a company's sales revenue (from that market) divided by the total sales revenue available in that market. It can also be expressed as a company's unit sales volume (in a market) divided by the total volume of units sold in that market.
   a. Market share
   b. Business-to-business
   c. Green marketing
   d. Marketing plan

2. _____ is a term applied in many countries to a reference interest rate used by banks. The term originally indicated the rate of interest at which banks lent to favored customers, i.e., those with high credibility, though this is no longer always the case. Some variable interest rates may be expressed as a percentage above or below _____.
   a. 1990 Clean Air Act
   b. Reserve requirement
   c. Lock box
   d. Prime rate

3. _____ refers to the movement of cash into or out of a business or financial product. It is usually measured during a specified, finite period of time. Measurement of _____ can be used

   - to determine a project's rate of return or value. The time of _____s into and out of projects are used as inputs in financial models such as internal rate of return, and net present value.
   - to determine problems with a business's liquidity. Being profitable does not necessarily mean being liquid. A company can fail because of a shortage of cash, even while profitable.
   - as an alternate measure of a business's profits when it is believed that accrual accounting concepts do not represent economic realities. For example, a company may be notionally profitable but generating little operational cash (as may be the case for a company that barters its products rather than selling for cash.) In such a case, the company may be deriving additional operating cash by issuing shares evaluating default risk, re-investment requirements, etc.

   _____ is a generic term used differently depending on the context. It may be defined by users for their own purposes.

   a. Sweat equity
   b. Gross profit margin
   c. Gross profit
   d. Cash flow

4. _____ is the point where a person stops employment completely. A person may also semi-retire and keep some sort of _____ job, out of choice rather than necessity. This usually happens upon reaching a determined age, when physical conditions don't allow the person to work any more (by illness or accident), or even for personal choice (usually in the presence of an adequate pension or personal savings.)
   a. Severance package
   b. Wrongful dismissal
   c. Termination of employment
   d. Retirement

5. _____ is the management of the flow of goods, information and other resources, including energy and people, between the point of origin and the point of consumption in order to meet the requirements of consumers (frequently, and originally, military organizations.) _____ involves the integration of information, transportation, inventory, warehousing, material-handling, and packaging, and occasionally security. _____ is a channel of the supply chain which adds the value of time and place utility.
   a. Logistics
   b. 1990 Clean Air Act
   c. 28-hour day
   d. Third-party logistics

Chapter 15. Sources of Debt Financing

6. A _____ is a business that is privately owned and operated, with a small number of employees and relatively low volume of sales. The legal definition of 'small' often varies by country and industry, but is generally under 100 employees in the United States and under 50 employees in the European Union. In comparison, the definition of mid-sized business by the number of employees is generally under 500 in the U.S. and 250 for the European Union.
   a. Critical Success Factor
   b. Golden Boot Compensation
   c. Small Business
   d. Pre-determined overhead rate

7. The _____ is a United States government agency that provides support to small businesses.

   The mission of the _____ is 'to maintain and strengthen the nation's economy by enabling the establishment and viability of small businesses and by assisting in the economic recovery of communities after disasters.'

   The _____ makes loans directly to businesses and acts as a guarantor on bank loans. In some circumstances it also makes loans to victims of natural disasters, works to get government procurement contracts for small businesses, and assists businesses with management, technical and training issues.
   a. 1990 Clean Air Act
   b. 28-hour day
   c. 33 Strategies of War
   d. Small Business Administration

8. A _____ is any credit source extended to a business by a bank or financial institution. A _____ may take several forms such as cash credit, overdraft, demand loan, export packing credit, term loan, discounting or purchase of commercial bills etc. It is like an account that can readily be tapped into if the need arises or not touched at all and saved for emergencies.
   a. 1990 Clean Air Act
   b. 28-hour day
   c. 33 Strategies of War
   d. Line of credit

9. Title _____s serve as guarantees to the recipient of property, ensuring that the recipient receives what he or she bargained for. The English _____s of title, sometimes included in deeds to real property, are that the grantor is lawfully seized (in fee simple) of the property, (2) that the grantor has the right to convey the property to the grantee, (3) that the property is conveyed without encumbrances (this _____ is frequently modified to allow for certain encumbrances), (4) that the grantor has done no act to encumber the property, (5) that the grantee shall have quiet possession of the property, and (6) that the grantor will execute such further assurances of the land as may be requisite (Nos. 3 and 4, which overlap significantly, are sometimes treated as one item.)
   a. Trade secret
   b. Business valuation
   c. Covenant
   d. Hostile work environment

10. In business and accounting, _____s are everything of value that is owned by a person or company. Any property or object of value that one possesses, usually considered as applicable to the payment of one's debts is considered an _____. Simplistically stated, _____s are things of value that can be readily converted into cash.
    a. AAAI
    b. A Stake in the Outcome
    c. Asset
    d. A4e

11. In financial accounting, a _____ or statement of financial position is a summary of a person's or organization's balances. Assets, liabilities and ownership equity are listed as of a specific date, such as the end of its financial year. A _____ is often described as a snapshot of a company's financial condition.

Chapter 15. Sources of Debt Financing

a. 1990 Clean Air Act
c. 33 Strategies of War
b. Balance sheet
d. 28-hour day

12. A _____ is a formal statement of a set of business goals, the reasons why they are believed attainable, and the plan for reaching those goals. It may also contain background information about the organization or team attempting to reach those goals.

The business goals may be defined for for-profit or for non-profit organizations.

a. Time management
c. Crisis management
b. Distributed management
d. Business plan

13. _____, commonly known as e-commerce, consists of the buying and selling of products or services over electronic systems such as the Internet and other computer networks. The amount of trade conducted electronically has grown extraordinarily with widespread Internet usage. The use of commerce is conducted in this way, spurring and drawing on innovations in electronic funds transfer, supply chain management, Internet marketing, online transaction processing, electronic data interchange (EDI), inventory management systems, and automated data collection systems.

a. Electronic Commerce
c. Online shopping
b. A4e
d. A Stake in the Outcome

14. _____ is one of a series of accounting transactions dealing with the billing of customers who owe money to a person, company or organization for goods and services that have been provided to the customer. In most business entities this is typically done by generating an invoice and mailing or electronically delivering it to the customer, who in turn must pay it within an established timeframe called credit or payment terms.

An example of a common payment term is Net 30, meaning payment is due in the amount of the invoice 30 days from the date of invoice.

a. Accumulated Depreciation
c. Other revenue
b. A Stake in the Outcome
d. Accounts receivable

15. _____ is a financial mechanism in which a debtor obtains the right to delay payments to a creditor, for a defined period of time, in exchange for a charge or fee. Essentially, the party that owes money in the present purchases the right to delay the payment until some future date. The discount, or charge, is simply the difference between the original amount owed in the present and the amount that has to be paid in the future to settle the debt.

a. Linear model
c. Ruin theory
b. Financial modeling
d. Discounting

16. _____ exists when one firm provides goods or services to a customer with an agreement to bill them later, or receive a shipment or service from a supplier under an agreement to pay them later. It can be viewed as an essential element of capitalization in an operating business because it can reduce the required capital investment to operate the business if it is managed properly. _____ is the largest use of capital for a majority of business to business (B2B) sellers in the United States and is a critical source of capital for a majority of all businesses.

a. Trade credit
c. 1990 Clean Air Act
b. Countertrade
d. Buy-sell agreement

Chapter 15. Sources of Debt Financing

17. _____ is a broad label that refers to any individuals or households that use goods and services generated within the economy. The concept of a _____ is used in different contexts, so that the usage and significance of the term may vary.

Typically when business people and economists talk of _____s they are talking about person as _____, an aggregated commodity item with little individuality other than that expressed in the buy/not-buy decision.

a. 28-hour day
b. 1990 Clean Air Act
c. 33 Strategies of War
d. Consumer

18. A _____ is a funding round of securities which are sold without a initial public offering, usually to a small number of chosen private investors. In the United States, these placements are not subject to the Securities Act of 1933 and do not have to be registered with the Securities and Exchange Commission, although the sale must conform to SEC rules. _____s may typically consist of stocks, shares or warrants and purchasers are often institutional investors such as banks, insurance companies or pension funds.

a. Labor intensive
b. Niche market
c. Choquet integral
d. Private placement

19. _____ is an advertisement in which a particular product specifically mentions a competitor by name for the express purpose of showing why the competitor is inferior to the product naming it.

This should not be confused with parody advertisements, where a fictional product is being advertised for the purpose of poking fun at the particular advertisement, nor should it be confused with the use of a coined brand name for the purpose of comparing the product without actually naming an actual competitor. ('Wikipedia tastes better and is less filling than the Encyclopedia Galactica.')

In the 1980s, during what has been referred to as the cola wars, soft-drink manufacturer Pepsi ran a series of advertisements where people, caught on hidden camera, in a blind taste test, chose Pepsi over rival Coca-Cola.

a. 1990 Clean Air Act
b. 28-hour day
c. 33 Strategies of War
d. Comparative advertising

20. _____ is the process of sharing of skills, knowledge, technologies, methods of manufacturing, samples of manufacturing and facilities among governments and other institutions to ensure that scientific and technological developments are accessible to a wider range of users who can then further develop and exploit the technology into new products, processes, applications, materials or services. It is closely related to (and may arguably be considered a subset of) Knowledge transfer. Related terms, used almost synonymously, include 'technology valorisation' and 'technology commercialisation'.

a. Mediation
b. Competition law
c. Technology Transfer
d. Munn v. Illinois

21. _____ is exchange of capital, goods, and services across international borders or territories. In most countries, it represents a significant share of gross domestic product (GDP.) While _____ has been present throughout much of history, its economic, social, and political importance has been on the rise in recent centuries.

Chapter 15. Sources of Debt Financing

a. AAAI
c. International trade
b. A Stake in the Outcome
d. A4e

22. _____ is a financial metric which represents operating liquidity available to a business. Along with fixed assets such as plant and equipment, _____ is considered a part of operating capital. It is calculated as current assets minus current liabilities.
   a. 28-hour day
   c. 33 Strategies of War
   b. 1990 Clean Air Act
   d. Working Capital

23. A _____ or transnational corporation is a corporation or enterprise that manages production or delivers services in more than one country. It can also be referred to as an international corporation.

The first modern _____ is generally thought to be the Dutch East India Company, established in 1602.

   a. Command center
   c. Multinational corporation
   b. Financial Accounting Standards Board
   d. Small and medium enterprises

24. _____ is a diversified financial services company with operations around the world. Wells Fargo is the fourth largest bank in the US by assets and the second largest bank by market cap.
   a. Committee for Economic Development
   c. Holding company
   b. Process-based management
   d. Wells Fargo ' Co.

25. _____ generally refers to a list of all planned expenses and revenues. It is a plan for saving and spending. A _____ is an important concept in microeconomics, which uses a _____ line to illustrate the trade-offs between two or more goods.
   a. 28-hour day
   c. Budget
   b. 33 Strategies of War
   d. 1990 Clean Air Act

26. _____ according to Onuoha (2007) is the practice of starting new organizations or revitalizing mature organizations, particularly new businesses generally in response to identified opportunities. _____ is often a difficult undertaking, as a vast majority of new businesses fail. Entrepreneurial activities are substantially different depending on the type of organization that is being started.
   a. A4e
   c. A Stake in the Outcome
   b. AAAI
   d. Entrepreneurship

Chapter 16. Location, Layout, and Physical Facilities

1. _____ or _____ data refers to selected population characteristics as used in government, marketing or opinion research, or the _____ profiles used in such research. Note the distinction from the term 'demography' Commonly-used _____s include race, age, income, disabilities, mobility (in terms of travel time to work or number of vehicles available), educational attainment, home ownership, employment status, and even location.
   a. Adam Smith
   b. Abraham Harold Maslow
   c. Affiliation
   d. Demographic

2. _____ is an integrated communications-based process through which individuals and communities discover that existing and newly-identified needs and wants may be satisfied by the products and services of others.

   _____ is defined by the American _____ Association as the activity, set of institutions, and processes for creating, communicating, delivering, and exchanging offerings that have value for customers, clients, partners, and society at large. The term developed from the original meaning which referred literally to going to market, as in shopping, or going to a market to buy or sell goods or services.

   a. Disruptive technology
   b. Customer relationship management
   c. Market development
   d. Marketing

3. The _____ is the Cabinet department of the United States government concerned with promoting economic growth. It was originally created as the _____ and Labor on February 14, 1903. It was subsequently renamed to the Department of Commerce on March 4, 1913, and its bureaus and agencies specializing in labor were transferred to the new Department of Labor.
   a. A Stake in the Outcome
   b. A4e
   c. AAAI
   d. United States Department of Commerce

4. The National Association of Securities Dealers Automated Quotations known as _____, is an American stock exchange. It is the largest electronic screen-based equity securities trading market in the United States. With approximately 3,800 companies and corporations, it has more trading volume per hour than any other stock exchange in the world.
   a. 33 Strategies of War
   b. NASDAQ
   c. 1990 Clean Air Act
   d. 28-hour day

5. A _____ is a business that is privately owned and operated, with a small number of employees and relatively low volume of sales. The legal definition of 'small' often varies by country and industry, but is generally under 100 employees in the United States and under 50 employees in the European Union. In comparison, the definition of mid-sized business by the number of employees is generally under 500 in the U.S. and 250 for the European Union.
   a. Golden Boot Compensation
   b. Small Business
   c. Pre-determined overhead rate
   d. Critical Success Factor

6. In mainstream economic theories, the supply of labor is the number of total hours that workers wish to work at a given real wage rate. Realisticly, the _____ is a fuction of various factors within an economy. For instance, overpopulation increases the number of available workers driving down wages and can result in high unemployment.
   a. 28-hour day
   b. Labor supply
   c. 33 Strategies of War
   d. 1990 Clean Air Act

7. A _____ is a compensation, usually financial, received by a worker in exchange for their labor.

Chapter 16. Location, Layout, and Physical Facilities

Compensation in terms of _____s is given to worker and compensation in terms of salary is given to employees. Compensation is a monetary benefits given to employees in returns of the services provided by them.

a. Profit-sharing agreement
c. Performance-related pay
b. State Compensation Insurance Fund
d. Wage

8. _____, commonly known as e-commerce, consists of the buying and selling of products or services over electronic systems such as the Internet and other computer networks. The amount of trade conducted electronically has grown extraordinarily with widespread Internet usage. The use of commerce is conducted in this way, spurring and drawing on innovations in electronic funds transfer, supply chain management, Internet marketing, online transaction processing, electronic data interchange (EDI), inventory management systems, and automated data collection systems.

a. Electronic Commerce
c. A Stake in the Outcome
b. A4e
d. Online shopping

9. The term '_____' refers to the concept of collecting information and attempting to spot a pattern in the information. In some fields of study, the term '_____' has more formally-defined meanings.

In project management _____ is a mathematical technique that uses historical results to predict future outcome.

a. Trend analysis
c. Least squares
b. Stepwise regression
d. Regression analysis

10. In economics, business, retail, and accounting, a _____ is the value of money that has been used up to produce something, and hence is not available for use anymore. In economics, a _____ is an alternative that is given up as a result of a decision. In business, the _____ may be one of acquisition, in which case the amount of money expended to acquire it is counted as _____.

a. Cost
c. Cost allocation
b. Cost overrun
d. Fixed costs

11. _____ , also referred to simply as a 'public offering' or 'flotation,' is when a company issues common stock or shares to the public for the first time. They are often issued by smaller, younger companies seeking capital to expand, but can also be done by large privately-owned companies looking to become publicly traded.

In an _____ the issuer may obtain the assistance of an underwriting firm, which helps it determine what type of security to issue (common or preferred), best offering price and time to bring it to market.

a. Outsourcing
c. Initial public offering
b. Unemployment insurance
d. Occupational Safety and Health Administration

Chapter 16. Location, Layout, and Physical Facilities

12. _____ is a form of communication that typically attempts to persuade potential customers to purchase or to consume more of a particular brand of product or service. 'While now central to the contemporary global economy and the reproduction of global production networks, it is only quite recently that _____ has been more than a marginal influence on patterns of sales and production. The formation of modern _____ was intimately bound up with the emergence of new forms of monopoly capitalism around the end of the 19th and beginning of the 20th century as one element in corporate strategies to create, organize and where possible control markets, especially for mass produced consumer goods.

a. A4e
b. A Stake in the Outcome
c. AAAI
d. Advertising

13. _____ is an advertisement in which a particular product specifically mentions a competitor by name for the express purpose of showing why the competitor is inferior to the product naming it.

This should not be confused with parody advertisements, where a fictional product is being advertised for the purpose of poking fun at the particular advertisement, nor should it be confused with the use of a coined brand name for the purpose of comparing the product without actually naming an actual competitor. ('Wikipedia tastes better and is less filling than the Encyclopedia Galactica.')

In the 1980s, during what has been referred to as the cola wars, soft-drink manufacturer Pepsi ran a series of advertisements where people, caught on hidden camera, in a blind taste test, chose Pepsi over rival Coca-Cola.

a. 1990 Clean Air Act
b. 28-hour day
c. 33 Strategies of War
d. Comparative advertising

14. _____ generally refers to a list of all planned expenses and revenues. It is a plan for saving and spending. A _____ is an important concept in microeconomics, which uses a _____ line to illustrate the trade-offs between two or more goods.

a. 1990 Clean Air Act
b. 28-hour day
c. 33 Strategies of War
d. Budget

15. _____ refers to increasing the spiritual, political, social or economic strength of individuals and communities. It often involves the empowered developing confidence in their own capacities.

The term Human _____ covers a vast landscape of meanings, interpretations, definitions and disciplines ranging from psychology and philosophy to the highly commercialized Self-Help industry and Motivational sciences.

a. A4e
b. Empowerment
c. A Stake in the Outcome
d. AAAI

16. _____ are programs designed to accelerate the successful development of entrepreneurial companies through an array of business support resources and services, developed and orchestrated by incubator management and offered both in the incubator and through its network of contacts. Incubators vary in the way they deliver their services, in their organizational structure, and in the types of clients they serve. Successful completion of a business incubation program increases the likelihood that a start-up company will stay in business for the long term: Historically, 87% of incubator graduates stay in business.

a. 1990 Clean Air Act
b. 28-hour day
c. 33 Strategies of War
d. Business incubators

17. The _____ of 1990 (ADA) is the short title of United States (Pub.L. 101-336, 104 Stat. 327, enacted July 26, 1990), codified at 42 U.S.C. Â§ 12101 et seq. It was signed into law on July 26, 1990, by President George H. W. Bush, and later amended with changes effective January 1, 2009. The ADA is a wide-ranging civil rights law that prohibits, under certain circumstances, discrimination based on disability. It affords similar protections against discrimination to Americans with disabilities as the Civil Rights Act of 1964,
a. Employment discrimination
b. Australian labour law
c. Equal Pay Act of 1963
d. Americans with Disabilities Act

18. _____s is the science of designing the job, equipment, and workplace to fit the worker. Proper _____ design is necessary to prevent repetitive strain injuries, which can develop over time and can lead to long-term disability.

_____s is concerned with the 'fit' between people and their work.

a. A4e
b. A Stake in the Outcome
c. AAAI
d. Ergonomic

19. A _____ is one scenario provided for evaluation by respondents in a Choice Experiment. Responses are collected and used to create a Choice Model. Respondents are usually provided with a series of differing _____s for evaluation.
a. Pairwise comparison
b. Computerized classification test
c. Thurstone scale
d. Choice Set

Chapter 17. Supply Chain Management

1. A _____ is the system of organizations, people, technology, activities, information and resources involved in moving a product or service from supplier to customer. _____ activities transform natural resources, raw materials and components into a finished product that is delivered to the end customer. In sophisticated _____ systems, used products may re-enter the _____ at any point where residual value is recyclable.

   a. Supply chain
   c. Wholesalers

   b. Drop shipping
   d. Packaging

2. _____ is the management of a network of interconnected businesses involved in the ultimate provision of product and service packages required by end customers (Harland, 1996.) _____ spans all movement and storage of raw materials, work-in-process inventory, and finished goods from point of origin to point of consumption (supply chain.)

   The definition an American professional association put forward is that _____ encompasses the planning and management of all activities involved in sourcing, procurement, conversion, and logistics management activities.

   a. Drop shipping
   c. Supply chain management

   b. Freight forwarder
   d. Packaging

3. _____ is a Japanese philosophy that focuses on continuous improvement throughout all aspects of life. When applied to the workplace, _____ activities continually improve all functions of a business, from manufacturing to management and from the CEO to the assembly line workers. By improving standardized activities and processes, _____ aims to eliminate waste.

   a. Sensitivity analysis
   c. Cross-docking

   b. Kaizen
   d. Psychological pricing

4. _____ is a business management strategy, initially implemented by Motorola, that today enjoys widespread application in many sectors of industry.

   _____ seeks to improve the quality of process outputs by identifying and removing the causes of defects (errors) and variation in manufacturing and business processes. It uses a set of quality management methods, including statistical methods, and creates a special infrastructure of people within the organization ('Black Belts' etc.)

   a. Theory of constraints
   c. Six Sigma

   b. Takt time
   d. Production line

5. _____ is a business management strategy aimed at embedding awareness of quality in all organizational processes. _____ has been widely used in manufacturing, education, hospitals, call centers, government, and service industries, as well as NASA space and science programs.

   As defined by the International Organization for Standardization (ISO):

   '_____ is a management approach for an organization, centered on quality, based on the participation of all its members and aiming at long-term success through customer satisfaction, and benefits to all members of the organization and to society.' ISO 8402:1994

Chapter 17. Supply Chain Management

One major aim is to reduce variation from every process so that greater consistency of effort is obtained. (Royse, D., Thyer, B., Padgett D., ' Logan T., 2006)

a. Total quality management
b. Quality management
c. 28-hour day
d. 1990 Clean Air Act

6. _____ can be considered to have three main components: quality control, quality assurance and quality improvement. _____ is focused not only on product quality, but also the means to achieve it. _____ therefore uses quality assurance and control of processes as well as products to achieve more consistent quality.

a. Quality management
b. Total quality management
c. 28-hour day
d. 1990 Clean Air Act

7. _____ is the process of comparing the cost, cycle time, productivity, or quality of a specific process or method to another that is widely considered to be an industry standard or best practice. Essentially, _____ provides a snapshot of the performance of your business and helps you understand where you are in relation to a particular standard. The result is often a business case for making changes in order to make improvements.

a. Cost leadership
b. Competitive heterogeneity
c. Complementors
d. Benchmarking

8. In neuroscience, the _____ is a collection of brain structures which attempts to regulate and control behavior by inducing pleasurable effects.

A psychological reward is a process that reinforces behavior -- something that, when offered, causes a behavior to increase in intensity. Reward is an operational concept for describing the positive value an individual ascribes to an object, behavioral act or an internal physical state.

a. 33 Strategies of War
b. 28-hour day
c. 1990 Clean Air Act
d. Reward system

9. _____ is an effective method of monitoring a process through the use of control charts. Control charts enable the use of objective criteria for distinguishing background variation from events of significance based on statistical techniques. Much of its power lies in the ability to monitor both process center and its variation about that center.

a. Quality control
b. Statistical process control
c. Process capability
d. Single Minute Exchange of Die

10. _____ is one of the managerial functions like planning, organizing, staffing and directing. It is an important function because it helps to check the errors and to take the corrective action so that deviation from standards are minimized and stated goals of the organization are achieved in desired manner. According to modern concepts, _____ is a foreseeing action whereas earlier concept of _____ was used only when errors were detected. _____ in management means setting standards, measuring actual performance and taking corrective action.

a. Turnover
b. Schedule of reinforcement
c. Decision tree pruning
d. Control

Chapter 17. Supply Chain Management

11. In probability theory, a probability distribution is called _____ if its cumulative distribution function is _____. This is equivalent to saying that for random variables X with the distribution in question, Pr[X = a] = 0 for all real numbers a, i.e.: the probability that X attains the value a is zero, for any number a. If the distribution of X is _____ then X is called a _____ random variable.

   a. Pay Band
   b. Connectionist expert systems
   c. Decision tree pruning
   d. Continuous

12. _____ is a management process whereby delivery (customer valued) processes are constantly evaluated and improved in the light of their efficiency, effectiveness and flexibility.

Some see it as a meta process for most management systems (Business Process Management, Quality Management, Project Management). Deming saw it as part of the 'system' whereby feedback from the process and customer were evaluated against organisational goals.

   a. Critical Success Factor
   b. First-mover advantage
   c. Sole proprietorship
   d. Continuous Improvement Process

13. _____ is the level of inventory that minimizes the total inventory holding costs and ordering costs. The framework used to determine this order quantity is also known as Wilson _____ Model. The model was developed by F. W. Harris in 1913.

   a. Event management
   b. Effective executive
   c. Anti-leadership
   d. Economic order quantity

14. In economics, business, retail, and accounting, a _____ is the value of money that has been used up to produce something, and hence is not available for use anymore. In economics, a _____ is an alternative that is given up as a result of a decision. In business, the _____ may be one of acquisition, in which case the amount of money expended to acquire it is counted as _____.

   a. Fixed costs
   b. Cost allocation
   c. Cost overrun
   d. Cost

15. In business management, _____ is money spent to keep and maintain a stock of goods in storage.

The most obvious _____s include rent for the required space; equipment, materials, and labor to operate the space; insurance; security; interest on money invested in the inventory and space, and other direct expenses. Some stored goods become obsolete before they are sold, reducing their contribution to revenue while having no effect on their _____.

   a. Market niche
   b. Choquet integral
   c. Private placement
   d. Holding cost

16. The _____ of a product is the cost per standard unit supplied, which may be a single sample or a container of a given number. When purchasing more than a single unit, the total cost will increase with the number of units, but it is common for the _____ to decrease as quantity is increased (bulk purchasing), as there are discounts etc. This reduction in long run _____s which arise from an increase in production/purchasing is due to the fixed costs being spread out over more products and is called economies of scale.

Chapter 17. Supply Chain Management

a. Unit cost
b. AAAI
c. A4e
d. A Stake in the Outcome

17. _____ is a form of communication that typically attempts to persuade potential customers to purchase or to consume more of a particular brand of product or service. 'While now central to the contemporary global economy and the reproduction of global production networks, it is only quite recently that _____ has been more than a marginal influence on patterns of sales and production. The formation of modern _____ was intimately bound up with the emergence of new forms of monopoly capitalism around the end of the 19th and beginning of the 20th century as one element in corporate strategies to create, organize and where possible control markets, especially for mass produced consumer goods.

a. AAAI
b. A4e
c. A Stake in the Outcome
d. Advertising

18. In economics, and cost accounting, _____ describes the total economic cost of production and is made up of variable costs, which vary according to the quantity of a good produced and include inputs such as labor and raw materials, plus fixed costs, which are independent of the quantity of a good produced and include inputs (capital) that cannot be varied in the short term, such as buildings and machinery. _____ in economics includes the total opportunity cost of each factor of production in addition to fixed and variable costs.

The rate at which _____ changes as the amount produced changes is called marginal cost.

a. 1990 Clean Air Act
b. 33 Strategies of War
c. 28-hour day
d. Total cost

19. _____ is one of a series of accounting transactions dealing with the billing of customers who owe money to a person, company or organization for goods and services that have been provided to the customer. In most business entities this is typically done by generating an invoice and mailing or electronically delivering it to the customer, who in turn must pay it within an established timeframe called credit or payment terms.

An example of a common payment term is Net 30, meaning payment is due in the amount of the invoice 30 days from the date of invoice.

a. Accumulated Depreciation
b. Accounts receivable
c. A Stake in the Outcome
d. Other revenue

20. The _____ is the level of inventory when a fresh order should be made with suppliers to bring the inventory up by the Economic order quantity ('EOQ'.)

The _____ for replenishment of stock occurs when the level of inventory drops down to zero. In view of instantaneous replenishment of stock the level of inventory jumps to the original level from zero level.

a. 1990 Clean Air Act
b. Finished goods
c. 28-hour day
d. Reorder point

21. In economics, _____ is the desire to own something and the ability to pay for it. The term _____ signifies the ability or the willingness to buy a particular commodity at a given point of time.

Chapter 17. Supply Chain Management

a. 33 Strategies of War
b. Demand
c. 28-hour day
d. 1990 Clean Air Act

22. _____ is a term used by inventory specialists to describe a level of extra stock that is maintained below the cycle stock to buffer against stockouts. _____ exists to counter uncertainties in supply and demand. _____ is defined as extra units of inventory carried as protection against possible stockouts .(shortfall in raw material or packaging.)

a. Process automation
b. Product life cycle
c. Safety stock
d. Knowledge worker

23. _____ is an advertisement in which a particular product specifically mentions a competitor by name for the express purpose of showing why the competitor is inferior to the product naming it.

This should not be confused with parody advertisements, where a fictional product is being advertised for the purpose of poking fun at the particular advertisement, nor should it be confused with the use of a coined brand name for the purpose of comparing the product without actually naming an actual competitor. ('Wikipedia tastes better and is less filling than the Encyclopedia Galactica.')

In the 1980s, during what has been referred to as the cola wars, soft-drink manufacturer Pepsi ran a series of advertisements where people, caught on hidden camera, in a blind taste test, chose Pepsi over rival Coca-Cola.

a. 33 Strategies of War
b. 28-hour day
c. 1990 Clean Air Act
d. Comparative advertising

24. _____ measures the performance of a system. Certain goals are defined and the _____ gives the percentage to which they should be achieved.

Examples

- Percentage of calls answered in a call center.
- Percentage of customers waiting less than a given fixed time.
- Percentage of customers that do not experience a stock out.

_____ is used in supply chain management and in inventory management to measure the performance of inventory systems.

Under stochastic conditions it is unavoidable that in some periods the inventory on hand is not sufficient to deliver the complete demand and, as a consequence, that part of the demand is filled only after an inventory-related waiting time.

a. Service level
b. 33 Strategies of War
c. 1990 Clean Air Act
d. 28-hour day

Chapter 17. Supply Chain Management

25. _____-model (SCOR(r)) is a process reference model developed by the management consulting firm PRTM and AMR Research and endorsed by the Supply-Chain Council (SCC) as the cross-industry de facto standard diagnostic tool for supply chain management. SCOR enables users to address, improve, and communicate supply chain management practices within and between all interested parties in the Extended Enterprise.

SCOR(r) is a management tool, spanning from the supplier's supplier to the customer's customer. The model has been developed by the members of the Council on a volunteer basis to describe the business activities associated with all phases of satisfying a customer's demand.

 a. Supply chain management software
 b. Supply-Chain Operations Reference
 c. Supply Chain Risk Management
 d. Delayed differentiation

26. _____ , also referred to simply as a 'public offering' or 'flotation,' is when a company issues common stock or shares to the public for the first time. They are often issued by smaller, younger companies seeking capital to expand, but can also be done by large privately-owned companies looking to become publicly traded.

In an _____ the issuer may obtain the assistance of an underwriting firm, which helps it determine what type of security to issue (common or preferred), best offering price and time to bring it to market.

 a. Unemployment insurance
 b. Outsourcing
 c. Occupational Safety and Health Administration
 d. Initial public offering

27. _____ is an unconventional system of promotions that relies on time, energy and imagination rather than a big marketing budget. Typically, _____ tactics are unexpected and unconventional; consumers are targeted in unexpected places, which can make the idea that's being marketed memorable, generate buzz, and even spread virally. The term was coined and defined by Jay Conrad Levinson in his 1984 book _____.

 a. 28-hour day
 b. 1990 Clean Air Act
 c. Relationship marketing
 d. Guerrilla marketing

28. _____ is an integrated communications-based process through which individuals and communities discover that existing and newly-identified needs and wants may be satisfied by the products and services of others.

_____ is defined by the American _____ Association as the activity, set of institutions, and processes for creating, communicating, delivering, and exchanging offerings that have value for customers, clients, partners, and society at large. The term developed from the original meaning which referred literally to going to market, as in shopping, or going to a market to buy or sell goods or services.

 a. Market development
 b. Disruptive technology
 c. Customer relationship management
 d. Marketing

29. _____ is a recursive process where two or more people or organizations work together in an intersection of common goals -- for example, an intellectual endeavor that is creative in nature--by sharing knowledge, learning and building consensus. _____ does not require leadership and can sometimes bring better results through decentralization and egalitarianism. In particular, teams that work collaboratively can obtain greater resources, recognition and reward when facing competition for finite resources._____ is also present in opposing goals exhibiting the notion of adversarial _____, though this is not a common case for using the term.

a. Collectivism
c. 28-hour day
b. Collaboration
d. 1990 Clean Air Act

30. The phrase mergers and _____s refers to the aspect of corporate strategy, corporate finance and management dealing with the buying, selling and combining of different companies that can aid, finance, or help a growing company in a given industry grow rapidly without having to create another business entity.

An _____, also known as a takeover or a buyout, is the buying of one company (the 'target') by another. An _____ may be friendly or hostile.

a. A Stake in the Outcome
c. Acquisition
b. AAAI
d. A4e

31. In decision theory and estimation theory, the _____ of an estimator, $\hat{\theta}$, of an unknown parameter of the distribution, θ, is the expected value of the loss function

$$R(\theta, \hat{\theta}) = \mathbb{E}_\theta L(\theta, \hat{\theta}) = \int L(\theta, \hat{\theta}) \, dP_\theta.$$

where dP_θ is a probability measure parametrized by θ.

- For a scalar parameter θ and a quadratic loss function,

$$L(\theta, \hat{\theta}) = (\theta - \hat{\theta})^2$$

the _____ function becomes the mean squared error of the estimate,

$$R(\theta, \hat{\theta}) = E_\theta(\theta - \hat{\theta})^2$$

- In density estimation, the unknown parameter is probability density itself. The loss function is typically chosen to be a norm in an appropriate function space. For example, for L^2 norm,

$$L(f, \hat{f}) = \|f - \hat{f}\|_2^2$$

the _____ function becomes the mean integrated squared error

$$R(f, \hat{f}) = E\|f - \hat{f}\|^2$$

a. Linear model
b. Risk aversion
c. Financial modeling
d. Risk

Chapter 18. Managing Inventory

1. _____ is the process of estimation in unknown situations. Prediction is a similar, but more general term. Both can refer to estimation of time series, cross-sectional or longitudinal data.
   a. 33 Strategies of War
   b. Forecasting
   c. 1990 Clean Air Act
   d. 28-hour day

2. In economics, business, retail, and accounting, a _____ is the value of money that has been used up to produce something, and hence is not available for use anymore. In economics, a _____ is an alternative that is given up as a result of a decision. In business, the _____ may be one of acquisition, in which case the amount of money expended to acquire it is counted as _____.
   a. Fixed costs
   b. Cost overrun
   c. Cost
   d. Cost allocation

3. In business management, _____ is money spent to keep and maintain a stock of goods in storage.

The most obvious _____s include rent for the required space; equipment, materials, and labor to operate the space; insurance; security; interest on money invested in the inventory and space, and other direct expenses. Some stored goods become obsolete before they are sold, reducing their contribution to revenue while having no effect on their _____.

   a. Holding cost
   b. Market niche
   c. Private placement
   d. Choquet integral

4. The _____ is an equation that equals the cost of goods sold divided by the average inventory. Average inventory equals beginning inventory plus ending inventory divided by 2.

The formula for _____:

$$\boxed{} >$$

The formula for average inventory:

$$\boxed{} >$$

A low turnover rate may point to overstocking, obsolescence, or deficiencies in the product line or marketing effort.

   a. A4e
   b. A Stake in the Outcome
   c. Asset turnover
   d. Inventory turnover

5. _____ is a form of communication that typically attempts to persuade potential customers to purchase or to consume more of a particular brand of product or service. 'While now central to the contemporary global economy and the reproduction of global production networks, it is only quite recently that _____ has been more than a marginal influence on patterns of sales and production. The formation of modern _____ was intimately bound up with the emergence of new forms of monopoly capitalism around the end of the 19th and beginning of the 20th century as one element in corporate strategies to create, organize and where possible control markets, especially for mass produced consumer goods.

Chapter 18. Managing Inventory

a. A4e
b. AAAI
c. A Stake in the Outcome
d. Advertising

6. _____ is one of the managerial functions like planning, organizing, staffing and directing. It is an important function because it helps to check the errors and to take the corrective action so that deviation from standards are minimized and stated goals of the organization are achieved in desired manner. According to modern concepts, _____ is a foreseeing action whereas earlier concept of _____ was used only when errors were detected. _____ in management means setting standards, measuring actual performance and taking corrective action.

a. Turnover
b. Decision tree pruning
c. Schedule of reinforcement
d. Control

7. In a human resources context, _____ or labor _____ is the rate at which an employer gains and loses employees. Simple ways to describe it are 'how long employees tend to stay' or 'the rate of traffic through the revolving door.' _____ is measured for individual companies and for their industry as a whole. If an employer is said to have a high _____ relative to its competitors, it means that employees of that company have a shorter average tenure than those of other companies in the same industry.

a. Career portfolios
b. Continuous
c. Ten year occupational employment projection
d. Turnover

8. _____ is the use of an object (typically referred to as an RFID tag) applied to or incorporated into a product, animal, or person for the purpose of identification and tracking using radio waves. Some tags can be read from several meters away and beyond the line of sight of the reader.

Most RFID tags contain at least two parts.

a. 33 Strategies of War
b. 1990 Clean Air Act
c. Radio-frequency identification
d. 28-hour day

9. In probability theory, a probability distribution is called _____ if its cumulative distribution function is _____. This is equivalent to saying that for random variables X with the distribution in question, Pr[X = a] = 0 for all real numbers a, i.e.: the probability that X attains the value a is zero, for any number a. If the distribution of X is _____ then X is called a _____ random variable.

a. Continuous
b. Decision tree pruning
c. Pay Band
d. Connectionist expert systems

10. _____ is a management process whereby delivery (customer valued) processes are constantly evaluated and improved in the light of their efficiency, effectiveness and flexibility.

Some see it as a meta process for most management systems (Business Process Management, Quality Management, Project Management). Deming saw it as part of the 'system' whereby feedback from the process and customer were evaluated against organisational goals.

a. First-mover advantage
b. Sole proprietorship
c. Critical Success Factor
d. Continuous Improvement Process

Chapter 18. Managing Inventory

11. _____ is an inventory strategy that strives to improve the return on investment of a business by reducing in-process inventory and its associated carrying costs. To meet _____ objectives, the process relies on signals between different points in the process. This means the process is often driven by a series of signals, or Kanban , which tell production when to make the next part. Kanban are usually 'tickets' but can be simple visual signals, such as the presence or absence of a part on a shelf. Implemented correctly, _____ can dramatically improve a manufacturing organization's return on investment, quality, and efficiency.

   a. 1990 Clean Air Act
   b. 28-hour day
   c. 33 Strategies of War
   d. Just-in-time

12. _____ is a worldwide management consulting firm that focuses on solving issues of concern to senior management. McKinsey serves as an advisor to the world's leading businesses, governments, and institutions. It is widely recognized as a leader and one of the most prestigious firms in the management consulting industry.

   a. 1990 Clean Air Act
   b. McKinsey ' Company
   c. 33 Strategies of War
   d. 28-hour day

13. _____ refers to increasing the spiritual, political, social or economic strength of individuals and communities. It often involves the empowered developing confidence in their own capacities.

   The term Human _____ covers a vast landscape of meanings, interpretations, definitions and disciplines ranging from psychology and philosophy to the highly commercialized Self-Help industry and Motivational sciences.

   a. A4e
   b. A Stake in the Outcome
   c. AAAI
   d. Empowerment

14. _____ is an advertisement in which a particular product specifically mentions a competitor by name for the express purpose of showing why the competitor is inferior to the product naming it.

   This should not be confused with parody advertisements, where a fictional product is being advertised for the purpose of poking fun at the particular advertisement, nor should it be confused with the use of a coined brand name for the purpose of comparing the product without actually naming an actual competitor. ('Wikipedia tastes better and is less filling than the Encyclopedia Galactica.')

   In the 1980s, during what has been referred to as the cola wars, soft-drink manufacturer Pepsi ran a series of advertisements where people, caught on hidden camera, in a blind taste test, chose Pepsi over rival Coca-Cola.

   a. 28-hour day
   b. Comparative advertising
   c. 33 Strategies of War
   d. 1990 Clean Air Act

15. In accounting and auditing, _____ is defined as a process effected by an organization's structure, work and authority flows, people and management information systems, designed to help the organization accomplish specific goals or objectives. It is a means by which an organization's resources are directed, monitored, and measured. It plays an important role in preventing and detecting fraud and protecting the organization's resources, both physical (e.g., machinery and property) and intangible (e.g., reputation or intellectual property such as trademarks.)

a. Internal auditing
c. A Stake in the Outcome
b. Audit committee
d. Internal control

Chapter 19. Staffing and Leading a Growing Company

1. _____ has been described as the 'process of social influence in which one person can enlist the aid and support of others in the accomplishment of a common task'. A definition more inclusive of followers comes from Alan Keith of Genentech who said '_____ is ultimately about creating a way for people to contribute to making something extraordinary happen.'

_____ is one of the most salient aspects of the organizational context. However, defining _____ has been challenging.

a. Situational leadership
c. Leadership
b. 28-hour day
d. 1990 Clean Air Act

2. An _____ is a person who has possession of an enterprise and assumes significant accountability for the inherent risks and the outcome. It is an ambitious leader who combines land, labor, and capital to create and market new goods or services. The term is a loanword from French and was first defined by the Irish economist Richard Cantillon.

a. Entrepreneur
c. A4e
b. A Stake in the Outcome
d. AAAI

3. _____, also referred to simply as a 'public offering' or 'flotation,' is when a company issues common stock or shares to the public for the first time. They are often issued by smaller, younger companies seeking capital to expand, but can also be done by large privately-owned companies looking to become publicly traded.

In an _____ the issuer may obtain the assistance of an underwriting firm, which helps it determine what type of security to issue (common or preferred), best offering price and time to bring it to market.

a. Unemployment insurance
c. Outsourcing
b. Initial public offering
d. Occupational Safety and Health Administration

4. _____ is a mathematical science pertaining to the collection, analysis, interpretation or explanation, and presentation of data. It also provides tools for prediction and forecasting based on data. It is applicable to a wide variety of academic disciplines, from the natural and social sciences to the humanities, government and business.

a. Statistics
c. Failure rate
b. Location parameter
d. Simple moving average

5. _____ refers to various methodologies for analyzing the requirements of a job.

The general purpose of _____ is to document the requirements of a job and the work performed. Job and task analysis is performed as a basis for later improvements, including: definition of a job domain; describing a job; developing performance appraisals, selection systems, promotion criteria, training needs assessment, and compensation plans.

a. Work design
c. Management process
b. Hersey-Blanchard situational theory
d. Job analysis

6. A _____ is a list of the general tasks and responsibilities of a position. Typically, it also includes to whom the position reports, specifications such as the qualifications needed by the person in the job, salary range for the position, etc. A _____ is usually developed by conducting a job analysis, which includes examining the tasks and sequences of tasks necessary to perform the job.

Chapter 19. Staffing and Leading a Growing Company

a. Recruitment advertising
c. Recruitment

b. Job description
d. Recruitment Process Insourcing

7. The _____, commonly known as the DOT was the creation of the U.S. Employment Service, which used its thousands of occupational definitions to match job seekers to jobs from 1939 to the late 1990s.

Before 1939, nationwide occupational information was not conveniently reported by the Employment Service. By 1939, it had become clear to the Employment service that a standardized volume of job definitions was needed for employment-related purposes.

a. 1990 Clean Air Act
c. 28-hour day

b. Dictionary of Occupational Titles
d. 33 Strategies of War

8. A _____ is a process in which a potential employee is evaluated by an employer for prospective employment in their company, organization and was established in the late 16th century.

A _____ typically precedes the hiring decision, and is used to evaluate the candidate. The interview is usually preceded by the evaluation of submitted résumés from interested candidates, then selecting a small number of candidates for interviews.

a. Supported employment
c. Split shift

b. Job interview
d. Payrolling

9. The _____ is a Cabinet department of the United States government responsible for occupational safety, wage and hour standards, unemployment insurance benefits, re-employment services, and some economic statistics. Many U.S. states also have such departments. The department is headed by the United States Secretary of Labor.

a. A4e
c. United States Department of Labor

b. AAAI
d. A Stake in the Outcome

10. The _____ of 1990 (ADA) is the short title of United States (Pub.L. 101-336, 104 Stat. 327, enacted July 26, 1990), codified at 42 U.S.C. § 12101 et seq. It was signed into law on July 26, 1990, by President George H. W. Bush, and later amended with changes effective January 1, 2009. The ADA is a wide-ranging civil rights law that prohibits, under certain circumstances, discrimination based on disability. It affords similar protections against discrimination to Americans with disabilities as the Civil Rights Act of 1964,

a. Employment discrimination
c. Australian labour law

b. Equal Pay Act of 1963
d. Americans with Disabilities Act

11. A _____ or background investigation is the process of looking up and compiling criminal records, commercial records and financial records (in certain instances such as employment screening) of an individual.

_____s are often requested by employers on job candidates, especially on candidates seeking a position that requires high security or a position of trust, such as in a school, hospital, financial institution, airport, and government (including law enforcement and military.) These checks are traditionally administered by a government agency for a nominal fee, but can also be administered by private companies.

a. Malcolm Baldrige National Quality Award
b. Time and attendance
c. Background check
d. Labour productivity

12. _____ is a contract between two parties, one being the employer and the other being the employee. An employee may be defined as: 'A person in the service of another under any contract of hire, express or implied, oral or written, where the employer has the power or right to control and direct the employee in the material details of how the work is to be performed.' Black's Law Dictionary page 471 (5th ed. 1979.)

a. Employment rate
b. Exit interview
c. Employment
d. Employment counsellor

13. _____ is an advertisement in which a particular product specifically mentions a competitor by name for the express purpose of showing why the competitor is inferior to the product naming it.

This should not be confused with parody advertisements, where a fictional product is being advertised for the purpose of poking fun at the particular advertisement, nor should it be confused with the use of a coined brand name for the purpose of comparing the product without actually naming an actual competitor. ('Wikipedia tastes better and is less filling than the Encyclopedia Galactica.')

In the 1980s, during what has been referred to as the cola wars, soft-drink manufacturer Pepsi ran a series of advertisements where people, caught on hidden camera, in a blind taste test, chose Pepsi over rival Coca-Cola.

a. 1990 Clean Air Act
b. Comparative advertising
c. 33 Strategies of War
d. 28-hour day

14. An _____ is a mostly hierarchical concept of subordination of entities that collaborate and contribute to serve one common aim.

Organizations are a variant of clustered entities. The structure of an organization is usually set up in many a styles, dependent on their objectives and ambience.

a. Open shop
b. Informal organization
c. Organizational structure
d. Organizational development

15. The 'business case for _____', theorizes that in a global marketplace, a company that employs a diverse workforce (both men and women, people of many generations, people from ethnically and racially diverse backgrounds etc.) is better able to understand the demographics of the marketplace it serves and is thus better equipped to thrive in that marketplace than a company that has a more limited range of employee demographics.

An additional corollary suggests that a company that supports the _____ of its workforce can also improve employee satisfaction, productivity and retention.

a. Trademark
b. Kanban
c. Virtual team
d. Diversity

Chapter 19. Staffing and Leading a Growing Company

16. _____ is a type of thought exhibited by group members who try to minimize conflict and reach consensus without critically testing, analyzing, and evaluating ideas. Individual creativity, uniqueness, and independent thinking are lost in the pursuit of group cohesiveness, as are the advantages of reasonable balance in choice and thought that might normally be obtained by making decisions as a group. During _____, members of the group avoid promoting viewpoints outside the comfort zone of consensus thinking.

   a. Psychological statistics
   b. Self-report inventory
   c. Diffusion of responsibility
   d. Groupthink

17. _____ describes the situation when output from (or information about the result of) an event or phenomenon in the past will influence the same event/phenomenon in the present or future. When an event is part of a chain of cause-and-effect that forms a circuit or loop, then the event is said to 'feed back' into itself.

   _____ is also a synonym for:

   - _____ signal; the information about the initial event that is the basis for subsequent modification of the event.
   - _____ loop; the causal path that leads from the initial generation of the _____ signal to the subsequent modification of the event.

   _____ is a mechanism, process or signal that is looped back to control a system within itself. Such a loop is called a _____ loop.

   a. Feedback
   b. Feedback loop
   c. 1990 Clean Air Act
   d. Positive feedback

18. _____ is an international professional services company, whose main expertise is consultancy-based coaching and training. _____ is headquartered in Brussels, Belgium and has 25 offices in 16 countries.

   _____ International was founded by Eric _____ in 1971 in Switzerland.

   a. Karuna Institute
   b. National Occupational Standards
   c. Personal trainer
   d. Krauthammer

19. _____ refers to increasing the spiritual, political, social or economic strength of individuals and communities. It often involves the empowered developing confidence in their own capacities.

   The term Human _____ covers a vast landscape of meanings, interpretations, definitions and disciplines ranging from psychology and philosophy to the highly commercialized Self-Help industry and Motivational sciences.

   a. AAAI
   b. A Stake in the Outcome
   c. Empowerment
   d. A4e

20. The phrase mergers and _____s refers to the aspect of corporate strategy, corporate finance and management dealing with the buying, selling and combining of different companies that can aid, finance, or help a growing company in a given industry grow rapidly without having to create another business entity.

Chapter 19. Staffing and Leading a Growing Company

An _____, also known as a takeover or a buyout, is the buying of one company (the 'target') by another. An _____ may be friendly or hostile.

a. A Stake in the Outcome
b. A4e
c. AAAI
d. Acquisition

21. _____ refers to the methods of practicing and using another person's business philosophy. The franchisor grants the independent operator the right to distribute its products, techniques, and trademarks for a percentage of gross monthly sales and a royalty fee. Various tangibles and intangibles such as national or international advertising, training, and other support services are commonly made available by the franchisor.

a. 28-hour day
b. Franchising
c. ServiceMaster
d. 1990 Clean Air Act

22. A _____ is someone who helps a group of people understand their common objectives and assists them to plan to achieve them without taking a particular position in the discussion. The _____ will try to assist the group in achieving a consensus on any disagreements that preexist or emerge in the meeting so that it has a strong basis for future action. The role has been likened to that of a midwife who assists in the process of birth but is not the producer of the end result.

a. Facilitator
b. 1990 Clean Air Act
c. 33 Strategies of War
d. 28-hour day

23. A _____ is a name or trademark connected with a product or producer. _____s have become increasingly important components of culture and the economy, now being described as 'cultural accessories and personal philosophies'.

Some people distinguish the psychological aspect of a _____ from the experiential aspect.

a. Brand loyalty
b. Brand awareness
c. Brand extension
d. Brand

24. _____ is a management technique pioneered by Michael Phillips in San Francisco in the late '60's and early '70s. The concept's most visible success was by Jack Stack and his team at SRC Holdings and popularized in 1995 by John Case. The technique is to give employees all relevant financial information about the company so they can make better decisions as workers.

a. A Stake in the Outcome
b. A4e
c. AAAI
d. Open-book management

25. In organizational development (OD), _____ is the application of Socio-Technical Systems principles and techniques to the humanization of work.

The aims of _____ to improved job satisfaction, to improved through-put, to improved quality and to reduced employee problems, e.g., grievances, absenteeism.

Under scientific management people would be directed by reason and the problems of industrial unrest would be appropriately (i.e., scientifically) addressed.

Chapter 19. Staffing and Leading a Growing Company

a. Management process
c. Work design
b. Path-goal theory
d. Graduate recruitment

26. _____ means increasing the scope of a job through extending the range of its job duties and responsibilities. This contradicts the principles of specialisation and the division of labour whereby work is divided into small units, each of which is performed repetitively by an individual worker. Some motivational theories suggest that the boredom and alienation caused by the division of labour can actually cause efficiency to fall.
a. Delayering
c. Centralization
b. Mock interview
d. Job enlargement

27. _____ is an attempt to motivate employees by giving them the opportunity to use the range of their abilities. It is an idea that was developed by the American psychologist Frederick Herzberg in the 1950s. It can be contrasted to job enlargement which simply increases the number of tasks without changing the challenge.
a. C-A-K-E
c. Cash cow
b. Job enrichment
d. Catfish effect

28. _____ is an approach to management development where an individual is moved through a schedule of assignments designed to give him or her a breadth of exposure to the entire operation.

_____ is also practiced to allow qualified employees to gain more insights into the processes of a company, and to reduce boredom and increase job satisfaction through job variation.

The term _____ can also mean the scheduled exchange of persons in offices, especially in public offices, prior to the end of incumbency or the legislative period.

a. 33 Strategies of War
c. 28-hour day
b. 1990 Clean Air Act
d. Job rotation

29. In mathematical logic, _____ is a valid argument and rule of inference which makes the inference that, if the conjunction A and B is true, then A is true, and B is true.

In formal language:

$$A \wedge B \vdash A$$

or

$$A \wedge B \vdash B$$

The argument has one premise, namely a conjunction, and one often uses _____ in longer arguments to derive one of the conjuncts.

An example in English:

It's raining and it's pouring.

a. Validity
b. Fuzzy logic
c. 1990 Clean Air Act
d. Simplification

30. _____ is a company policy or program that enables employees to have more decision authority on where they will work regardless of time of day. For example, they may choose to work in the office or from home or from a client's office or even a caf>é.
a. 1990 Clean Air Act
b. 28-hour day
c. 33 Strategies of War
d. Flexplace

31. _____ is a variable work schedule, in contrast to traditional work arrangements requiring employees to work a standard 9am to 5pm day. Under _____, there is typically a core period of the day when employees are expected to be at work (for example, between 11 am and 3pm), while the rest of the working day is 'flexitime', in which employees can choose when they work, subject to achieving total daily, weekly or monthly hours in the region of what the employer expects, and subject to the necessary work being done.

A _____ policy allows staff to determine when they will work, while a flexplace policy allows staff to determine where they will work.

a. Fiduciary
b. Certificate of Incorporation
c. Bennett Amendment
d. Flextime

32. _____, e-commuting, e-work, telework, working from home (WFH), or working at home (WAH) is a work arrangement in which employees enjoy flexibility in working location and hours. In other words, the daily commute to a central place of work is replaced by telecommunication links. Many work from home, while others, occasionally also referred to as nomad workers or web commuters utilize mobile telecommunications technology to work from coffee shops or myriad other locations.
a. 28-hour day
b. 33 Strategies of War
c. 1990 Clean Air Act
d. Telecommuting

33. _____ is a method of supporting unassigned seating in an office environment. It is similar and is sometimes confused with hot desking, another method of supporting unassigned seating. _____ is reservation-based unassigned seating, whereas, hot desking is reservation-less unassigned seating.
a. 1990 Clean Air Act
b. 28-hour day
c. 33 Strategies of War
d. Hotelling

34. A _____ is someone engaging in recruitment, which is the solicitation of individuals to fill jobs or positions within any group, such as a corporation or sports team. _____s can be divided into two groups; those working internally for one organization, and those working for multiple clients in a third-party broker relationship, sometimes called headhunters or agency _____s.

Chapter 19. Staffing and Leading a Growing Company

An internal _____ is member of a company or organization and typically works in human resources (HR), which in the past was known as the Personnel Office, or just Personnel.

   a. 1990 Clean Air Act
   b. 28-hour day
   c. 33 Strategies of War
   d. Recruiter

35. A _____ is a compensation, usually financial, received by a worker in exchange for their labor.

Compensation in terms of _____s is given to worker and compensation in terms of salary is given to employees. Compensation is a monetary benefits given to employees in returns of the services provided by them.

   a. Profit-sharing agreement
   b. Performance-related pay
   c. State Compensation Insurance Fund
   d. Wage

36. _____ is a method by which the job performance of an employee is evaluated _____ is a part of career development.

_____s are regular reviews of employee performance within organizations

Generally, the aims of a _____ are to:

- Give feedback on performance to employees.
- Identify employee training needs.
- Document criteria used to allocate organizational rewards.
- Form a basis for personnel decisions: salary increases, promotions, disciplinary actions, etc.
- Provide the opportunity for organizational diagnosis and development.
- Facilitate communication between employee and administraton
- Validate selection techniques and human resource policies to meet federal Equal Employment Opportunity requirements.

A common approach to assessing performance is to use a numerical or scalar rating system whereby managers are asked to score an individual against a number of objectives/attributes. In some companies, employees receive assessments from their manager, peers, subordinates and customers while also performing a self assessment.

   a. Performance appraisal
   b. Progressive discipline
   c. Personnel management
   d. Human resource management

37. _____ is the process of subjecting an author's scholarly work, research, or ideas to the scrutiny of others who are experts in the same field. _____ requires a community of experts in a given field, who are qualified and able to perform impartial review. Impartial review, especially of work in less narrowly defined or inter-disciplinary fields, may be difficult to accomplish; and the significance of an idea may never be widely appreciated among its contemporaries.

   a. 1990 Clean Air Act
   b. Peer review
   c. 28-hour day
   d. 33 Strategies of War

Chapter 20. Management Succession and Risk Management Strategies in the Family Business

1. _____ is a form of communication that typically attempts to persuade potential customers to purchase or to consume more of a particular brand of product or service. 'While now central to the contemporary global economy and the reproduction of global production networks, it is only quite recently that _____ has been more than a marginal influence on patterns of sales and production. The formation of modern _____ was intimately bound up with the emergence of new forms of monopoly capitalism around the end of the 19th and beginning of the 20th century as one element in corporate strategies to create, organize and where possible control markets, especially for mass produced consumer goods.
    a. A Stake in the Outcome
    b. Advertising
    c. A4e
    d. AAAI

2. A _____ occurs when a financial sponsor acquires a controlling interest in a company's equity and where a significant percentage of the purchase price is financed through leverage (borrowing.) The assets of the acquired company are used as collateral for the borrowed capital, sometimes with assets of the acquiring company. The bonds or other paper issued for _____s are commonly considered not to be investment grade because of the significant risks involved.
    a. Venture capital
    b. Leveraged buyout
    c. Limited partners
    d. Growth capital

3. _____ is the process of disassembly and recovery at the module level and, eventually, at the component level. It requires the repair or replacement of worn out or obsolete components and modules. Parts subject to degradation affecting the performance or the expected life of the whole are replaced.
    a. Remanufacturing
    b. Productivity
    c. Capacity planning
    d. Methods-time measurement

4. A _____ is an investment transaction by which an entire company or a controlling part of the stock of a company is sold. A firm 'buys out' a company to take control of it. A _____ can take the form of a leveraged _____, a venture capital _____ or a management _____.
    a. Sweat equity
    b. Gross profit
    c. Buyout
    d. Shareholder value

5. _____ is the state or fact of exclusive rights and control over property, which may be an object, land/real estate or intellectual property. An _____ right is also referred to as title. The concept of _____ has existed for thousands of years and in all cultures.
    a. A Stake in the Outcome
    b. A4e
    c. Emanation of the state
    d. Ownership

6. _____ occurs when a corporation is owned in whole or in part by its employees. Employees are usually given a share of the corporation after a certain length of employment or they can buy shares at any time. A corporation owned entirely by its employees (such as a worker cooperative) will not, therefore, have its shares sold on public stock markets, often opting instead for mixed ownership arrangements involving a trust.
    a. Anaconda Copper
    b. Employee Ownership
    c. Amoco Corporation
    d. AT'T Inc.

7. _____ has been described as the 'process of social influence in which one person can enlist the aid and support of others in the accomplishment of a common task'. A definition more inclusive of followers comes from Alan Keith of Genentech who said '_____ is ultimately about creating a way for people to contribute to making something extraordinary happen.'

Chapter 20. Management Succession and Risk Management Strategies in the Family Business

_____ is one of the most salient aspects of the organizational context. However, defining _____ has been challenging.

a. 28-hour day
c. Leadership
b. Situational leadership
d. 1990 Clean Air Act

8. A _____ is typically created as part of an A/B Living trust estate plan after the death of the first spouse to die. During life, a married couple transfers ownership of property into a trust. Upon the death of the first party to die, the terms of the trust require that some portion of the property be transferred into 'TRUST A' and some other portion into 'TRUST B.' The first of these trusts, A, holds property that remains accessible to the surviving spouse during his or her life.

a. 28-hour day
c. 1990 Clean Air Act
b. Joint and several liability
d. Bypass trust

9. In business and accounting, _____s are everything of value that is owned by a person or company. Any property or object of value that one possesses, usually considered as applicable to the payment of one's debts is considered an _____. Simplistically stated, _____s are things of value that can be readily converted into cash.

a. AAAI
c. A4e
b. A Stake in the Outcome
d. Asset

10. A _____ is a form of partnership similar to a general partnership, except that in addition to one or more general partners (GPs), there are one or more limited partners (_____s.) It is a partnership in which only one partner is required to be a general partner.

The GPs are, in all major respects, in the same legal position as partners in a conventional firm, i.e. they have management control, share the right to use partnership property, share the profits of the firm in predefined proportions, and have joint and several liability for the debts of the partnership.

a. Pension fund
c. Growth capital
b. Private equity
d. Limited partnership

11. A _____ is a type of business entity in which partners (owners) share with each other the profits or losses of the business. _____s are often favored over corporations for taxation purposes, as the _____ structure does not generally incur a tax on profits before it is distributed to the partners (i.e. there is no dividend tax levied.) However, depending on the _____ structure and the jurisdiction in which it operates, owners of a _____ may be exposed to greater personal liability than they would as shareholders of a corporation.

a. Mediation
c. Due process
b. Federal Employers Liability Act
d. Partnership

12. In decision theory and estimation theory, the _____ of an estimator, $\hat{\theta}$, of an unknown parameter of the distribution, θ, is the expected value of the loss function

$$R(\theta, \hat{\theta}) = \mathbb{E}_\theta L(\theta, \hat{\theta}) = \int L(\theta, \hat{\theta}) \, dP_\theta.$$

where dP_θ is a probability measure parametrized by θ.

- For a scalar parameter θ and a quadratic loss function,

$$L(\theta, \hat{\theta}) = (\theta - \hat{\theta})^2$$

the _____ function becomes the mean squared error of the estimate,

$$R(\theta, \hat{\theta}) = E_\theta (\theta - \hat{\theta})^2$$

- In density estimation, the unknown parameter is probability density itself. The loss function is typically chosen to be a norm in an appropriate function space. For example, for L^2 norm,

$$L(f, \hat{f}) = \|f - \hat{f}\|_2^2$$

the _____ function becomes the mean integrated squared error

$$R(f, \hat{f}) = E\|f - \hat{f}\|^2$$

a. Financial modeling
b. Linear model
c. Risk aversion
d. Risk

13. _____ is the identification, assessment, and prioritization of risks followed by coordinated and economical application of resources to minimize, monitor, and control the probability and/or impact of unfortunate events.. Risks can come from uncertainty in financial markets, project failures, legal liabilities, credit risk, accidents, natural causes and disasters as well as deliberate attacks from an adversary. Several _____ standards have been developed including the Project Management Institute, the National Institute of Science and Technology, actuarial societies, and ISO standards.
    a. Kanban
    b. Succession planning
    c. Trademark
    d. Risk management

14. In economics, business, retail, and accounting, a _____ is the value of money that has been used up to produce something, and hence is not available for use anymore. In economics, a _____ is an alternative that is given up as a result of a decision. In business, the _____ may be one of acquisition, in which case the amount of money expended to acquire it is counted as _____.
    a. Cost overrun
    b. Cost allocation
    c. Fixed costs
    d. Cost

15. _____ is a way of expressing knowledge or belief that an event will occur or has occurred. In mathematics the concept has been given an exact meaning in _____ theory, that is used extensively in such areas of study as mathematics, statistics, finance, gambling, science, and philosophy to draw conclusions about the likelihood of potential events and the underlying mechanics of complex systems.

Chapter 20. Management Succession and Risk Management Strategies in the Family Business

The word _____ does not have a consistent direct definition.

a. Standard deviation
c. Time series analysis
b. Probability
d. Statistics

16. _____ plant, and equipment, is a term used in accountancy for assets and property which cannot easily be converted into cash. This can be compared with current assets such as cash or bank accounts, which are described as liquid assets. In most cases, only tangible assets are referred to as fixed.

a. 33 Strategies of War
c. 1990 Clean Air Act
b. Fixed asset
d. 28-hour day

17. _____ is an advertisement in which a particular product specifically mentions a competitor by name for the express purpose of showing why the competitor is inferior to the product naming it.

This should not be confused with parody advertisements, where a fictional product is being advertised for the purpose of poking fun at the particular advertisement, nor should it be confused with the use of a coined brand name for the purpose of comparing the product without actually naming an actual competitor. ('Wikipedia tastes better and is less filling than the Encyclopedia Galactica.')

In the 1980s, during what has been referred to as the cola wars, soft-drink manufacturer Pepsi ran a series of advertisements where people, caught on hidden camera, in a blind taste test, chose Pepsi over rival Coca-Cola.

a. 28-hour day
c. Comparative advertising
b. 33 Strategies of War
d. 1990 Clean Air Act

18. An _____ is a sum paid by A to B by way of compensation for a particular loss suffered by B. The indemnifying party (A) may or may not be responsible for the loss suffered by the indemnified party (B.) Forms of _____ include cash payments, repairs, replacement, and reinstatement.

In common parlance, _____ is often used as a synonym for compensation or reparation.

a. A4e
c. Indemnity
b. A Stake in the Outcome
d. AAAI

19. _____ is one of the managerial functions like planning, organizing, staffing and directing. It is an important function because it helps to check the errors and to take the corrective action so that deviation from standards are minimized and stated goals of the organization are achieved in desired manner.According to modern concepts, _____ is a foreseeing action whereas earlier concept of _____ was used only when errors were detected. _____ in management means setting standards, measuring actual performance and taking corrective action.

a. Decision tree pruning
c. Schedule of reinforcement
b. Turnover
d. Control

Chapter 20. Management Succession and Risk Management Strategies in the Family Business

20. _____ protects professional practitioners such as architects, home inspectors, lawyers, physicians, and accountants against potential negligence claims made by their patients/clients. _____ may take on different names depending on the profession. For example, _____ in reference to the medical profession may be called Medical Malpractice.

a. 1990 Clean Air Act
b. Workers compensation
c. 28-hour day
d. Professional liability insurance

21. The _____ of 1990 (ADA) is the short title of United States (Pub.L. 101-336, 104 Stat. 327, enacted July 26, 1990), codified at 42 U.S.C. § 12101 et seq. It was signed into law on July 26, 1990, by President George H. W. Bush, and later amended with changes effective January 1, 2009. The ADA is a wide-ranging civil rights law that prohibits, under certain circumstances, discrimination based on disability. It affords similar protections against discrimination to Americans with disabilities as the Civil Rights Act of 1964,

a. Employment discrimination
b. Equal Pay Act of 1963
c. Australian labour law
d. Americans with Disabilities Act

22. _____ is a contract between two parties, one being the employer and the other being the employee. An employee may be defined as: 'A person in the service of another under any contract of hire, express or implied, oral or written, where the employer has the power or right to control and direct the employee in the material details of how the work is to be performed.' Black's Law Dictionary page 471 (5th ed. 1979.)

a. Employment
b. Exit interview
c. Employment counsellor
d. Employment rate

23. The _____ is a United States labor law allowing an employee to take unpaid leave due to a serious health condition that makes the employee unable to perform his job or to care for a sick family member or to care for a new son or daughter (including by birth, adoption or foster care.) The bill was among the first signed into law by President Bill Clinton in his first term.

a. Sarbanes-Oxley Act of 2002
b. Harvester Judgment
c. Contributory negligence
d. Family and Medical Leave Act of 1993

24. An _____ details guidelines, expectations and procedures of a business or company to its employees.

_____s are given to employees on one of the first days of his/her job, in order to acquaint them with their new company and its policies.

Chapter 20. Management Succession and Risk Management Strategies in the Family Business 127

While it often varies from business to business, specific areas that an _____ may address include:

- A welcome statement, which may also briefly describe the company's history, reasons for its success and how the employee can contribute to future successes. It may also include a mission statement, or a statement about a business' goals and objectives.
- Orientation procedures. This usually involves providing a human resources manager or other designated employee completed income tax withholding forms, providing proof of identity and eligibility for employment (in accordance with the Immigration Reform and Control Act of 1986), proof of a completed drug test (by a designated medical center) and other required forms.
- Definitions of full- and part-time employment, and benefits each classification receives. In addition, this area also describes timekeeping procedures (such as defining a 'work week'.) This area may also include information about daily breaks (for lunch and rest.)
- Information about employee pay and benefits (such as vacation and insurance.) Usually, new employees are awarded some benefits, plus additional rewards (such as enrollment in a 401K retirement account program, additional vacation and pay raises) after having worked for a company for a certain period of time. These are spelled out in this section.
- Expectations about conduct and discipline policies. These sections include conduct policies for such areas as sexual harassment, alcohol and drug use, and attendance; plus, grounds for dismissal (i.e., getting fired) and due process. This area may also include information about filing grievances with supervisors and/or co-workers, and communicating work-related issues with supervisors and/or company managers.
- Guidelines for employee performance reviews (such as how and when they are conducted.)
- Policies for promotion or demotion to a certain position.
- Rules concerning mail; use of the telephone, company equipment, Internet and e-mail; and employee use of motor vehicles for job assignments.
- Procedures on handling on-the-job accidents, such as those that result in injury.
- How an employee may voluntarily terminate his job (through retirement or resignation), and exit interviews.
- A requirement that employees keep certain business information confidential. This area usually includes information about releasing employee records and information, as well as who may retrieve and inspect the information.

If the employer is covered by the Family and Medical Leave Act of 1993 - generally 50 or more employees - a handbook must have information about FMLA.

New employees are usually required to sign a form stating they have read and understand the information, and accept the terms of the _____.

a. Employment
c. Employee handbook
b. Informational interview
d. Underemployment

25. A _____ is a business that is privately owned and operated, with a small number of employees and relatively low volume of sales. The legal definition of 'small' often varies by country and industry, but is generally under 100 employees in the United States and under 50 employees in the European Union. In comparison, the definition of mid-sized business by the number of employees is generally under 500 in the U.S. and 250 for the European Union.

a. Pre-determined overhead rate
b. Critical Success Factor
c. Golden Boot Compensation
d. Small Business

26. In queueing theory, _____ is the proportion of the system's resources which is used by the traffic which arrives at it. It should be strictly less than one for the system to function well. It is usually represented by the symbol ρ.
   a. AAAI
   b. A Stake in the Outcome
   c. A4e
   d. Utilization

27. The general definition of an _____ is an evaluation of a person, organization, system, process, project or product. _____s are performed to ascertain the validity and reliability of information; also to provide an assessment of a system's internal control. The goal of an _____ is to express an opinion on the person / organization/system (etc) in question, under evaluation based on work done on a test basis.
   a. A Stake in the Outcome
   b. Internal control
   c. Audit committee
   d. Audit

Chapter 21. Ethics and Social Responsibility: Doing the Right Thing

1. The _____ captures an expanded spectrum of values and criteria for measuring organizational success: economic, ecological and social. With the ratification of the United Nations and ICLEI _____ standard for urban and community accounting in early 2007, this became the dominant approach to public sector full cost accounting. Similar UN standards apply to natural capital and human capital measurement to assist in measurements required by _____, e.g. the ecoBudget standard for reporting ecological footprint.
   - a. 1990 Clean Air Act
   - b. 28-hour day
   - c. 33 Strategies of War
   - d. Triple bottom line

2. _____ are a set of documents that describe an organization's policies for operation and the procedures necessary to fulfill the policies. They are often initiated because of some external requirement, such as environmental compliance or other governmental regulations, such as the American Sarbanes-Oxley Act requiring full openness in accounting practices. The easiest way to start writing _____ is to interview the users of the _____ and create a flow chart or task map or work flow of the process from start to finish.
   - a. Horizontal integration
   - b. Group booking
   - c. Customer retention
   - d. Policies and procedures

3. An _____ is any party that makes an investment.

The term has taken on a specific meaning in finance to describe the particular types of people and companies that regularly purchase equity or debt securities for financial gain in exchange for funding an expanding company. Less frequently, the term is applied to parties who purchase real estate, currency, commodity derivatives, personal property, or other assets.

   - a. A4e
   - b. Investor
   - c. AAAI
   - d. A Stake in the Outcome

4. In game theory, an _____ is a set of moves or strategies taken by the players, or their payoffs resulting from the actions or strategies taken by all players. The two are complementary in that given knowledge of the set of strategies of all players, the final state of the game is known, as are any relevant payoffs. In a game where chance or a random event is involved, the _____ is not known from only the set of strategies, but is only realized when the random event(s) are realized.
   - a. AAAI
   - b. A4e
   - c. Outcome
   - d. A Stake in the Outcome

5. _____, also referred to simply as a 'public offering' or 'flotation,' is when a company issues common stock or shares to the public for the first time. They are often issued by smaller, younger companies seeking capital to expand, but can also be done by large privately-owned companies looking to become publicly traded.

In an _____ the issuer may obtain the assistance of an underwriting firm, which helps it determine what type of security to issue (common or preferred), best offering price and time to bring it to market.

   - a. Occupational Safety and Health Administration
   - b. Initial public offering
   - c. Outsourcing
   - d. Unemployment insurance

Chapter 21. Ethics and Social Responsibility: Doing the Right Thing

6. _____ is an idea in the field of Organizational studies and management which describes the psychology, attitudes, experiences, beliefs and Values (personal and cultural values) of an organization. It has been defined as 'the specific collection of values and norms that are shared by people and groups in an organization and that control the way they interact with each other and with stakeholders outside the organization.'

This definition continues to explain organizational values also known as 'beliefs and ideas about what kinds of goals members of an organization should pursue and ideas about the appropriate kinds or standards of behavior organizational members should use to achieve these goals. From organizational values develop organizational norms, guidelines or expectations that prescribe appropriate kinds of behavior by employees in particular situations and control the behavior of organizational members towards one another.'

_____ is not the same as corporate culture.

a. Organizational development
b. Union shop
c. Organizational effectiveness
d. Organizational culture

7. _____ refers to the process of screening, and selecting qualified people for a job at an organization or firm mid- and large-size organizations and companies often retain professional recruiters or outsource some of the process to _____ agencies. External _____ is the process of attracting and selecting employees from outside the organization.

The _____ industry has four main types of agencies: employment agencies, _____ websites and job search engines, 'headhunters' for executive and professional _____, and in-house _____.

a. Labour hire
b. Recruitment Process Outsourcing
c. Recruitment
d. Referral recruitment

8. _____ in its literal sense is the process of transformation of local or regional phenomena into global ones. It can be described as a process by which the people of the world are unified into a single society and function together.

This process is a combination of economic, technological, sociocultural and political forces.

a. Cost Management
b. Collaborative Planning, Forecasting and Replenishment
c. Histogram
d. Globalization

9. _____ is a concept in ethics with several meanings. It is often used synonymously with such concepts as responsibility, answerability, enforcement, blameworthiness, liability and other terms associated with the expectation of account-giving. As an aspect of governance, it has been central to discussions related to problems in both the public and private (corporation) worlds.

a. A4e
b. A Stake in the Outcome
c. Usury
d. Accountability

Chapter 21. Ethics and Social Responsibility: Doing the Right Thing

10. The general definition of an _____ is an evaluation of a person, organization, system, process, project or product. _____s are performed to ascertain the validity and reliability of information; also to provide an assessment of a system's internal control. The goal of an _____ is to express an opinion on the person / organization/system (etc) in question, under evaluation based on work done on a test basis.

   a. A Stake in the Outcome
   b. Audit
   c. Internal control
   d. Audit committee

11. _____ according to Onuoha (2007) is the practice of starting new organizations or revitalizing mature organizations, particularly new businesses generally in response to identified opportunities. _____ is often a difficult undertaking, as a vast majority of new businesses fail. Entrepreneurial activities are substantially different depending on the type of organization that is being started.

   a. AAAI
   b. A4e
   c. A Stake in the Outcome
   d. Entrepreneurship

12. The 'business case for _____', theorizes that in a global marketplace, a company that employs a diverse workforce (both men and women, people of many generations, people from ethnically and racially diverse backgrounds etc.) is better able to understand the demographics of the marketplace it serves and is thus better equipped to thrive in that marketplace than a company that has a more limited range of employee demographics.

   An additional corollary suggests that a company that supports the _____ of its workforce can also improve employee satisfaction, productivity and retention.

   a. Diversity
   b. Trademark
   c. Virtual team
   d. Kanban

13. A _____ is the belief that there is a technique, method, process, activity, incentive or reward that is more effective at delivering a particular outcome than any other technique, method, process, etc. The idea is that with proper processes, checks, and testing, a desired outcome can be delivered with fewer problems and unforeseen complications. _____s can also be defined as the most efficient (least amount of effort) and effective (best results) way of accomplishing a task, based on repeatable procedures that have proven themselves over time for large numbers of people.

   a. Hierarchical organization
   b. Design management
   c. Fix it twice
   d. Best Practice

14. _____ has been described as the 'process of social influence in which one person can enlist the aid and support of others in the accomplishment of a common task'. A definition more inclusive of followers comes from Alan Keith of Genentech who said '_____ is ultimately about creating a way for people to contribute to making something extraordinary happen.'

   _____ is one of the most salient aspects of the organizational context. However, defining _____ has been challenging.

   a. 1990 Clean Air Act
   b. 28-hour day
   c. Situational leadership
   d. Leadership

Chapter 21. Ethics and Social Responsibility: Doing the Right Thing

15. The _____ of 1990 (ADA) is the short title of United States (Pub.L. 101-336, 104 Stat. 327, enacted July 26, 1990), codified at 42 U.S.C. § 12101 et seq. It was signed into law on July 26, 1990, by President George H. W. Bush, and later amended with changes effective January 1, 2009. The ADA is a wide-ranging civil rights law that prohibits, under certain circumstances, discrimination based on disability. It affords similar protections against discrimination to Americans with disabilities as the Civil Rights Act of 1964,

   a. Equal Pay Act of 1963   b. Employment discrimination
   c. Australian labour law   d. Americans with Disabilities Act

16. _____ and benefits in kind are various non-wage compensations provided to employees in addition to their normal wages or salaries. Where an employee exchanges (cash) wages for some other form of benefit, this is generally referred to as a 'salary sacrifice' arrangement. In most countries, most kinds of _____ are taxable to at least some degree.

   a. A4e   b. A Stake in the Outcome
   c. Interactive Accommodation Process   d. Employee benefits

17. The _____ was a landmark piece of legislation in the United States that outlawed racial segregation in schools, public places, and employment.

   a. Financial Security Law of France   b. Design patent
   c. Negligence in employment   d. Civil Rights Act of 1964

18. _____ indicates a more-or-less equal exchange or substitution of goods or services. English speakers often use the term to mean 'a favour for a favour' and the phrases with almost identical meaning include: 'what for what,' 'give and take,' 'tit for tat', 'this for that', and 'you scratch my back, and I'll scratch yours'.

In legal usage, _____ indicates that an item or a service has been traded in return for something of value, usually when the propriety or equity of the transaction is in question.

   a. 28-hour day   b. 1990 Clean Air Act
   c. 33 Strategies of War   d. Quid pro quo

19. _____ is unwelcome harassment of a sexual nature, or based upon the receiving party's sex or gender. In some contexts or circumstances, _____ may be illegal. It includes a range of behavior from seemingly mild transgressions and annoyances to actual sexual abuse or sexual assault.

   a. Sexual harassment   b. 28-hour day
   c. Hypernorms   d. 1990 Clean Air Act

20. The _____ is a United States statute that was passed in response to a series of United States Supreme Court decisions which limited the rights of employees who had sued their employers for discrimination. The Act represented the first effort since the passage of the Civil Rights Act of 1964 to modify some of the basic procedural and substantive rights provided by federal law in employment discrimination cases. It provided for the right to trial by jury on discrimination claims and introduced the possibility of emotional distress damages, while limiting the amount that a jury could award

The 1991 Act combined elements from two different civil rights acts of the past: the Civil Rights Act of 1866, better known by the number assigned to it in the codification of federal laws as 'Section 1981', and the employment-related provisions of the Civil Rights Act of 1964, generally referred to as 'Title VII', its location within the Act.

a. Resource Conservation and Recovery Act
b. Covenant
c. Negligence in employment
d. Civil Rights Act of 1991

21. The _____ is an independent agency of the United States government, established in 1914 by the _____ Act. Its principal mission is the promotion of 'consumer protection' and the elimination and prevention of what regulators perceive to be harmfully 'anti-competitive' business practices, such as coercive monopoly.

The _____ Act was one of President Wilson's major acts against trusts.

a. 1990 Clean Air Act
b. 33 Strategies of War
c. 28-hour day
d. Federal Trade Commission

22. _____ consists of the mental process of thinking involved with the process of judging the merits of multiple options and selecting one of them for action. Some simple examples include deciding whether to get up in the morning or go back to sleep, or selecting a given route for a journey. More complex examples (often decisions that affect what a person thinks or their core beliefs) include choosing a lifestyle, religious affiliation, or political position.

a. Trade study
b. Groups decision making
c. Championship mobilization
d. Choice

23. The _____ requires the Federal government to investigate and pursue trusts, companies and organizations suspected of violating the Act. It was the first United States Federal statute to limit cartels and monopolies, and today still forms the basis for most antitrust litigation by the federal government.

a. Sherman Antitrust Act
b. 28-hour day
c. 33 Strategies of War
d. 1990 Clean Air Act

24. _____ is the strategic and coherent approach to the management of an organisation's most valued assets - the people working there who individually and collectively contribute to the achievement of the objectives of the business. The terms '_____' and 'human resources' (HR) have largely replaced the term 'personnel management' as a description of the processes involved in managing people in organizations. In simple sense, _____ means employing people, developing their resources, utilizing, maintaining and compensating their services in tune with the job and organizational requirement.

a. Human Resource Management
b. Progressive discipline
c. Job knowledge
d. Revolving door syndrome

Chapter 22. The Legal Environment: Business Law and Government Regulation

1. _____ are paid to compensate the claimant for loss, injury, or harm suffered by another's breach of duty.

On a breach of contract by a defendant, a court generally awards the sum which would restore the injured party to the economic position that he or she expected from performance of the promise or promises .

When it is either not possible or desirable to award damages measured in that way, a court may award money damages designed to restore the injured party to the economic position that he or she had occupied at the time the contract was entered, or designed to prevent the breaching party from being unjustly enriched

a. 28-hour day
b. Compensatory damages
c. 33 Strategies of War
d. 1990 Clean Air Act

2. In finance, an _____ is a contract between a buyer and a seller that gives the buyer the right--but not the obligation--to buy or to sell a particular asset (the underlying asset) at a later day at an agreed price. In return for granting the _____, the seller collects a payment (the premium) from the buyer. A call _____ gives the buyer the right to buy the underlying asset; a put _____ gives the buyer of the _____ the right to sell the underlying asset.

a. AAAI
b. A Stake in the Outcome
c. Option
d. A4e

3. A _____ is a process in which a potential employee is evaluated by an employer for prospective employment in their company, organization and was established in the late 16th century.

A _____ typically precedes the hiring decision, and is used to evaluate the candidate. The interview is usually preceded by the evaluation of submitted résumés from interested candidates, then selecting a small number of candidates for interviews.

a. Supported employment
b. Split shift
c. Payrolling
d. Job interview

4. The _____, first published in 1952, is one of a number of uniform acts that have been promulgated in conjunction with efforts to harmonize the law of sales and other commercial transactions in all 50 states within the United States of America. This objective is deemed important because of the prevalence of commercial transactions that extend beyond one state (for example, where the goods are manufactured in state A, warehoused in state B, sold from state C and delivered in state D.) The _____ deals primarily with transactions involving personal property (movable property), not real property (immovable property.)

a. AAAI
b. Uniform Commercial Code
c. A4e
d. A Stake in the Outcome

5. _____ is Latin for 'Let the buyer beware'. Generally _____ is the property law doctrine that controls the sale of real property after the date of closing.

Under the doctrine of _____, the buyer could not recover from the seller for defects on the property that rendered the property unfit for ordinary purposes. The only exception was if the seller actively concealed latent defects. The modern trend in the US, however, is one of the Implied Warranty of Fitness that applies only to the sale of new residential housing by a builder-seller and the rule of _____ applies to all other sale situations.

Chapter 22. The Legal Environment: Business Law and Government Regulation

a. 1990 Clean Air Act
c. 28-hour day
b. 33 Strategies of War
d. Caveat emptor

6. An _____ is quite usually a standard guarantee from the seller of a product that specifies the extent to which the quality or performance of the product is assured and states the conditions under which the product can be returned, replaced, or repaired. It is often given in the form of a specific, written 'Warranty' document. However, a warranty may also arise by operation of law based upon the seller's description of the goods, and perhaps their source and quality, and any material deviation from that specification would violate the guarantee.
a. AAAI
c. A Stake in the Outcome
b. A4e
d. Express warranty

7. _____ is the area of law in which manufacturers, distributors, suppliers, retailers, and others who make products available to the public are held responsible for the injuries those products cause.

In the United States, the claims most commonly associated with _____ are negligence, strict liability, breach of warranty, and various consumer protection claims. The majority of _____ laws are determined at the state level and vary widely from state to state.

a. Right-to-work laws
c. Product liability
b. Leave of absence
d. Railway Labor Act

8. _____ is a legal concept in the common law legal systems usually used to achieve compensation for injuries (not accidents.) _____ is a type of tort or delict (also known as a civil wrong.)
a. Mediation
c. Diminishing returns
b. Certificate of Incorporation
d. Negligence

9. _____ are legal property rights over creations of the mind, both artistic and commercial, and the corresponding fields of law. Under _____ law, owners are granted certain exclusive rights to a variety of intangible assets, such as musical, literary, and artistic works; ideas, discoveries and inventions; and words, phrases, symbols, and designs. Common types of _____ include copyrights, trademarks, patents, industrial design rights and trade secrets.
a. Intent
c. Equal Pay Act
b. Intellectual property
d. Unemployment Action Center

10. _____ makes a person responsible for the damage and loss caused by his/her acts and omissions regardless of culpability. _____ is important in torts (especially product liability), corporations law, and criminal law.
a. Historiometry
c. Ten year occupational employment projection
b. Competency-based job descriptions
d. Strict liability

11. _____ plant, and equipment, is a term used in accountancy for assets and property which cannot easily be converted into cash. This can be compared with current assets such as cash or bank accounts, which are described as liquid assets. In most cases, only tangible assets are referred to as fixed.
a. Fixed asset
c. 1990 Clean Air Act
b. 33 Strategies of War
d. 28-hour day

12. A _____ is a set of exclusive rights granted by a state to an inventor or his assignee for a limited period of time in exchange for a disclosure of an invention.

The procedure for granting _____s, the requirements placed on the _____ee and the extent of the exclusive rights vary widely between countries according to national laws and international agreements. Typically, however, a _____ application must include one or more claims defining the invention which must be new, inventive, and useful or industrially applicable.

a. Federal Trade Commission Act
b. Labor Management Reporting and Disclosure Act
c. Food, Drug, and Cosmetic Act
d. Patent

13. A _____ is a distinctive sign or indicator used by an individual, business organization, or other legal entity to identify that the products and/or services to consumers with which the _____ appears originate from a unique source and to distinguish its products or services from those of other entities.

a. Succession planning
b. Trademark
c. Kanban
d. Virtual team

14. _____ is an advertisement in which a particular product specifically mentions a competitor by name for the express purpose of showing why the competitor is inferior to the product naming it.

This should not be confused with parody advertisements, where a fictional product is being advertised for the purpose of poking fun at the particular advertisement, nor should it be confused with the use of a coined brand name for the purpose of comparing the product without actually naming an actual competitor. ('Wikipedia tastes better and is less filling than the Encyclopedia Galactica.')

In the 1980s, during what has been referred to as the cola wars, soft-drink manufacturer Pepsi ran a series of advertisements where people, caught on hidden camera, in a blind taste test, chose Pepsi over rival Coca-Cola.

a. 28-hour day
b. 1990 Clean Air Act
c. 33 Strategies of War
d. Comparative advertising

15. A _____ is a relatively new executive level position at a corporation, company, organization typically reporting directly to the CEO or board of directors. The _____ is responsible for a brand's image, experience, and promise, and propagating it throughout all aspects of the company. The brand officer oversees marketing, advertising, design, public relations and customer service departments.

a. Chief executive officer
b. Director of communications
c. Purchasing manager
d. Chief brand officer

16. _____ is a legally declared inability or impairment of ability of an individual or organization to pay its creditors. Creditors may file a _____ petition against a debtor ('involuntary _____') in an effort to recoup a portion of what they are owed or initiate a restructuring. In the majority of cases, however, _____ is initiated by the debtor (a 'voluntary _____' that is filed by the insolvent individual or organization.)

a. 33 Strategies of War
b. 1990 Clean Air Act
c. Bankruptcy
d. 28-hour day

Chapter 22. The Legal Environment: Business Law and Government Regulation

17. In law, _____ refers to the process by which a company (or part of a company) is brought to an end, and the assets and property of the company redistributed. _____ can also be referred to as winding-up or dissolution, although dissolution technically refers to the last stage of _____. The process of _____ also arises when customs, an authority or agency in a country responsible for collecting and safeguarding customs duties, determines the final computation or ascertainment of the duties or drawback accruing on an entry.

a. 28-hour day
b. 1990 Clean Air Act
c. 33 Strategies of War
d. Liquidation

18. _____ , also referred to simply as a 'public offering' or 'flotation,' is when a company issues common stock or shares to the public for the first time. They are often issued by smaller, younger companies seeking capital to expand, but can also be done by large privately-owned companies looking to become publicly traded.

In an _____ the issuer may obtain the assistance of an underwriting firm, which helps it determine what type of security to issue (common or preferred), best offering price and time to bring it to market.

a. Unemployment insurance
b. Outsourcing
c. Occupational Safety and Health Administration
d. Initial public offering

19. The _____ was a regulatory body in the United States created by the Interstate Commerce Act of 1887, which was signed into law by President Grover Cleveland. The agency was abolished in 1995, and the agency's remaining functions were transferred to the Surface Transportation Board.

The Commission's five members were appointed by the President with the consent of the United States Senate.

a. American Institute of Industrial Engineers
b. United States Department of Agriculture
c. Extended Enterprise
d. Interstate Commerce Commission

20. _____ exists when sales of identical goods or services are transacted at different prices from the same provider. In a theoretical market with perfect information, no transaction costs or prohibition on secondary exchange (or re-selling) to prevent arbitrage, _____ can only be a feature of monopoly and oligopoly markets, where market power can be exercised. Otherwise, the moment the seller tries to sell the same good at different prices, the buyer at the lower price can arbitrage by selling to the consumer buying at the higher price but with a tiny discount.

a. Price discrimination
b. Price points
c. Target costing
d. Pricing objectives

21. The _____ requires the Federal government to investigate and pursue trusts, companies and organizations suspected of violating the Act. It was the first United States Federal statute to limit cartels and monopolies, and today still forms the basis for most antitrust litigation by the federal government.

a. Sherman Antitrust Act
b. 1990 Clean Air Act
c. 33 Strategies of War
d. 28-hour day

22. _____ is a broad label that refers to any individuals or households that use goods and services generated within the economy. The concept of a _____ is used in different contexts, so that the usage and significance of the term may vary.

Chapter 22. The Legal Environment: Business Law and Government Regulation

Typically when business people and economists talk of _____s they are talking about person as _____, an aggregated commodity item with little individuality other than that expressed in the buy/not-buy decision.

a. 28-hour day
b. 1990 Clean Air Act
c. Consumer
d. 33 Strategies of War

23. _____ laws are designed to ensure fair competition and the free flow of truthful information in the marketplace. The laws are designed to prevent businesses that engage in fraud or specified unfair practices from gaining an advantage over competitors and may provide additional protection for the weak and unable to take care of themselves. _____ laws are a form of government regulation which protects the interests of consumers.

a. Comprehensive Environmental Response, Compensation, and Liability Act
b. Sarbanes-Oxley Act
c. Certificate of Incorporation
d. Consumer protection

24. The _____ is an independent agency of the United States government, established in 1914 by the _____ Act. Its principal mission is the promotion of 'consumer protection' and the elimination and prevention of what regulators perceive to be harmfully 'anti-competitive' business practices, such as coercive monopoly.

The _____ Act was one of President Wilson's major acts against trusts.

a. Federal Trade Commission
b. 33 Strategies of War
c. 28-hour day
d. 1990 Clean Air Act

25. The _____ of 1914 (15 U.S.C Â§Â§ 41-58, as amended) established the Federal Trade Commission (FTC), a bipartisan body of five members appointed by the President of the United States for seven year terms. This Commission was authorized to issue Cease and Desist orders to large corporations to curb unfair trade practices. This Act also gave more flexibility to the US congress for judicial matters.

a. Sarbanes-Oxley Act of 2002
b. Resource Conservation and Recovery Act
c. Comprehensive Environmental Response, Compensation, and Liability Act
d. Federal Trade Commission Act

26. The _____ of 1936 (or Anti-Price Discrimination Act, 15 U.S.C. Â§ 13) is a United States federal law that prohibits what were considered, at the time of passage, to be anticompetitive practices by producers, specifically price discrimination. It grew out of practices in which chain stores were allowed to purchase goods at lower prices than other retailers.

a. Bona fide occupational qualification
b. Labor Management Reporting and Disclosure Act
c. Privity
d. Robinson-Patman Act

27. _____ is a form of communication that typically attempts to persuade potential customers to purchase or to consume more of a particular brand of product or service. 'While now central to the contemporary global economy and the reproduction of global production networks, it is only quite recently that _____ has been more than a marginal influence on patterns of sales and production. The formation of modern _____ was intimately bound up with the emergence of new forms of monopoly capitalism around the end of the 19th and beginning of the 20th century as one element in corporate strategies to create, organize and where possible control markets, especially for mass produced consumer goods.

Chapter 22. The Legal Environment: Business Law and Government Regulation

a. AAAI
c. A4e
b. A Stake in the Outcome
d. Advertising

28. In retail sales, a _____ is a form of fraud in which the party putting forth the fraud lures in customers by advertising a product or service at an unprofitably low price, then reveals to potential customers that the advertised good is not available but that a substitute is. This term has lots of other meanings, even outside of the marketing sense.

The goal of the _____ is to convince some buyers to purchase the substitute good as a means of avoiding disappointment over not getting the bait, or as a way to recover sunk costs expended to try to obtain the bait.

a. Bait and switch
c. 1990 Clean Air Act
b. 33 Strategies of War
d. 28-hour day

29. The _____ is a US law that applies to labels on many consumer products. It requires the label to state:

- The identity of the product;
- The name and place of business of the manufacturer, packer, or distributor; and
- The net quantity of contents.

The contents statement must include both metric and U.S. customary units.

Passed under Lyndon B. Johnson in 1966, the law first took effect on July 1, 1967. The metric labeling requirement was added in 1992 and took effect on February 14, 1994.

a. 1990 Clean Air Act
c. 33 Strategies of War
b. Fair Packaging and Labeling Act
d. 28-hour day

30. The _____ of June 30, 1906 is a United States federal law that provided federal inspection of meat products and forbade the manufacture, sale, or transportation of adulterated food products and poisonous patent medicines. The Act arose due to public education and expos>és from Muckrakers such as Upton Sinclair and Samuel Hopkins Adams, social activist Florence Kelley, researcher Harvey W. Wiley, and President Theodore Roosevelt.

The _____ was initially concerned with ensuring products were labeled correctly.

a. Public Utility Holding Company Act
c. 28-hour day
b. 1990 Clean Air Act
d. Pure Food and Drug Act

31. The _____ is an agency of the United States Department of Health and Human Services and is responsible for regulating and supervising the safety of foods, dietary supplements, drugs, vaccines, biological medical products, blood products, medical devices, radiation-emitting devices, veterinary products, and cosmetics. The FDA also enforces section 361 of the Public Health Service Act and the associated regulations, including sanitation requirements on interstate travel as well as specific rules for control of disease on products ranging from pet turtles to semen donations for assisted reproductive medicine techniques.

The FDA is an agency within the United States Department of Health and Human Services responsible for protecting and promoting the nation's public health.

Chapter 22. The Legal Environment: Business Law and Government Regulation

a. 1990 Clean Air Act
b. 33 Strategies of War
c. Food and Drug Administration
d. 28-hour day

32. _____ is the science, art and technology of enclosing or protecting products for distribution, storage, sale, and use. _____ also refers to the process of design, evaluation, and production of packages. _____ can be described as a coordinated system of preparing goods for transport, warehousing, logistics, sale, and end use.

a. Packaging
b. Supply chain management
c. Wholesalers
d. Supply chain

33. The phrase mergers and _____s refers to the aspect of corporate strategy, corporate finance and management dealing with the buying, selling and combining of different companies that can aid, finance, or help a growing company in a given industry grow rapidly without having to create another business entity.

An _____, also known as a takeover or a buyout, is the buying of one company (the 'target') by another. An _____ may be friendly or hostile.

a. AAAI
b. Acquisition
c. A Stake in the Outcome
d. A4e

34. _____ is a method of direct marketing in which a salesperson solicits to prospective customers to buy products or services, either over the phone or through a subsequent face to face or Web conferencing appointment scheduled during the call.

_____ can also include recorded sales pitches programmed to be played over the phone via automatic dialing. _____ has come under fire in recent years, being viewed as an annoyance by many.

a. 28-hour day
b. 33 Strategies of War
c. 1990 Clean Air Act
d. Telemarketing

35. The _____ of 1968 is a United States federal law designed to protect consumers in credit transactions, by requiring clear disclosure of key terms of the lending arrangement and all costs. The statute is contained in Title I of the Consumer Credit Protection Act, as amended (15 U.S.C. Â§ 1601 et seq.).

a. Fair Credit Reporting Act
b. Truth in Lending Act
c. 28-hour day
d. 1990 Clean Air Act

36. The United States _____ is an independent agency of the United States government created in 1972 through the Consumer Product Safety Act to protect 'against unreasonable risks of injuries associated with consumer products.' As of 2006 its acting chairman is Nancy Nord, a Republican. The other commissioner is Thomas Hill Moore, a Democrat. Normally the board has three commissioners.

a. 33 Strategies of War
b. 1990 Clean Air Act
c. 28-hour day
d. Consumer Product Safety Commission

37. A _____ is a formal statement of a set of business goals, the reasons why they are believed attainable, and the plan for reaching those goals. It may also contain background information about the organization or team attempting to reach those goals.

Chapter 22. The Legal Environment: Business Law and Government Regulation

The business goals may be defined for for-profit or for non-profit organizations.

a. Distributed management
c. Business plan
b. Time management
d. Crisis management

38. _____ refers to the movement of cash into or out of a business or financial product. It is usually measured during a specified, finite period of time. Measurement of _____ can be used

- to determine a project's rate of return or value. The time of _____s into and out of projects are used as inputs in financial models such as internal rate of return, and net present value.
- to determine problems with a business's liquidity. Being profitable does not necessarily mean being liquid. A company can fail because of a shortage of cash, even while profitable.
- as an alternate measure of a business's profits when it is believed that accrual accounting concepts do not represent economic realities. For example, a company may be notionally profitable but generating little operational cash (as may be the case for a company that barters its products rather than selling for cash.) In such a case, the company may be deriving additional operating cash by issuing shares evaluating default risk, re-investment requirements, etc.

_____ is a generic term used differently depending on the context. It may be defined by users for their own purposes.

a. Gross profit margin
c. Cash flow
b. Gross profit
d. Sweat equity

39. The term _____ has attracted attention in recent years in combination with the field of design management. In practice design managers within companies oftern operate in the field of _____ and design leaders in the field of design management. However, the tem _____ can not be equated entirely with design management and the terms are not interchangeable.

a. Design management
c. PDCA
b. Workflow
d. Design Leadership

40. _____, commonly known as e-commerce, consists of the buying and selling of products or services over electronic systems such as the Internet and other computer networks. The amount of trade conducted electronically has grown extraordinarily with widespread Internet usage. The use of commerce is conducted in this way, spurring and drawing on innovations in electronic funds transfer, supply chain management, Internet marketing, online transaction processing, electronic data interchange (EDI), inventory management systems, and automated data collection systems.

a. Electronic Commerce
c. A Stake in the Outcome
b. Online shopping
d. A4e

41. _____ refers to the methods of practicing and using another person's business philosophy. The franchisor grants the independent operator the right to distribute its products, techniques, and trademarks for a percentage of gross monthly sales and a royalty fee. Various tangibles and intangibles such as national or international advertising, training, and other support services are commonly made available by the franchisor.

a. Franchising
c. 28-hour day
b. 1990 Clean Air Act
d. ServiceMaster

Chapter 22. The Legal Environment: Business Law and Government Regulation

42. _____ is an unconventional system of promotions that relies on time, energy and imagination rather than a big marketing budget. Typically, _____ tactics are unexpected and unconventional; consumers are targeted in unexpected places, which can make the idea that's being marketed memorable, generate buzz, and even spread virally. The term was coined and defined by Jay Conrad Levinson in his 1984 book _____.

a. 28-hour day
b. Guerrilla marketing
c. Relationship marketing
d. 1990 Clean Air Act

43. _____ has been described as the 'process of social influence in which one person can enlist the aid and support of others in the accomplishment of a common task'. A definition more inclusive of followers comes from Alan Keith of Genentech who said '_____ is ultimately about creating a way for people to contribute to making something extraordinary happen.'

_____ is one of the most salient aspects of the organizational context. However, defining _____ has been challenging.

a. 28-hour day
b. Situational leadership
c. 1990 Clean Air Act
d. Leadership

44. _____ is one of the four Ps of the marketing mix. The other three aspects are product, promotion, and place. It is also a key variable in microeconomic price allocation theory.

a. Price floor
b. Transfer pricing
c. Penetration pricing
d. Pricing

45. A _____ is the system of organizations, people, technology, activities, information and resources involved in moving a product or service from supplier to customer. _____ activities transform natural resources, raw materials and components into a finished product that is delivered to the end customer. In sophisticated _____ systems, used products may re-enter the _____ at any point where residual value is recyclable.

a. Drop shipping
b. Supply chain
c. Wholesalers
d. Packaging

46. _____ is the management of a network of interconnected businesses involved in the ultimate provision of product and service packages required by end customers (Harland, 1996.) _____ spans all movement and storage of raw materials, work-in-process inventory, and finished goods from point of origin to point of consumption (supply chain.)

The definition an American professional association put forward is that _____ encompasses the planning and management of all activities involved in sourcing, procurement, conversion, and logistics management activities.

a. Freight forwarder
b. Packaging
c. Drop shipping
d. Supply chain management

47. _____ is an integrated communications-based process through which individuals and communities discover that existing and newly-identified needs and wants may be satisfied by the products and services of others.

Chapter 22. The Legal Environment: Business Law and Government Regulation

_____ is defined by the American _____ Association as the activity, set of institutions, and processes for creating, communicating, delivering, and exchanging offerings that have value for customers, clients, partners, and society at large. The term developed from the original meaning which referred literally to going to market, as in shopping, or going to a market to buy or sell goods or services.

a. Disruptive technology
b. Marketing
c. Market development
d. Customer relationship management

48. A _____ is a written document that details the necessary actions to achieve one or more marketing objectives. It can be for a product or service, a brand, or a product line. _____s cover between one and five years.
a. Marketing plan
b. Disruptive technology
c. Market development
d. Marketing strategy

49. The _____ is the primary federal law in the United States governing water pollution. The act established the symbolic goals of eliminating releases to water of high amounts of toxic substances, eliminating additional water pollution by 1985, and ensuring that surface waters would meet standards necessary for human sports and recreation by 1983.

The principal body of law currently in effect is based on the Federal Water Pollution Control Amendments of 1972, which significantly expanded and strengthened earlier legislation.

a. Foreign Corrupt Practices Act
b. Regulatory compliance
c. Non-disclosure agreement
d. Clean Water Act

50. Superfund is the common name for the _____, a United States federal law designed to clean up abandoned hazardous waste sites. Superfund provides broad federal authority to clean up releases or threatened releases of hazardous substances that may endanger public health or the environment. The law authorized the Environmental Protection Agency (EPA) to identify parties responsible for contamination of sites and compel the parties to clean up the sites.

a. Flextime
b. Comprehensive Environmental Response, Compensation, and Liability Act
c. Partnership
d. Munn v. Illinois

ANSWER KEY

Chapter 1
1. b   2. d   3. d   4. c   5. d   6. d   7. a   8. d   9. d   10. b
11. d   12. c   13. d   14. d   15. d   16. c   17. c   18. b   19. d   20. c

Chapter 2
1. b   2. d   3. d   4. d   5. d   6. a   7. d   8. c   9. b   10. c
11. d   12. d   13. b   14. b   15. a   16. c   17. a   18. b   19. a   20. d
21. a   22. d   23. d   24. d   25. d   26. a   27. d   28. d   29. a   30. b
31. a   32. d   33. d

Chapter 3
1. b   2. a   3. b   4. d   5. a   6. b   7. c   8. d   9. a   10. b
11. d   12. c   13. d   14. a   15. d   16. c   17. a   18. c   19. d   20. d
21. d   22. c   23. d   24. b   25. d   26. b   27. b   28. b   29. b   30. d
31. c   32. c   33. d   34. c   35. a   36. d   37. d

Chapter 4
1. b   2. b   3. a   4. d   5. d   6. d   7. b   8. a   9. a   10. d
11. d   12. d   13. b   14. d   15. d   16. d   17. a   18. d   19. c   20. d
21. d   22. a   23. d   24. c   25. a   26. c   27. d

Chapter 5
1. d   2. d   3. b   4. a   5. c   6. c   7. b   8. a   9. a   10. b
11. d   12. c   13. d   14. d   15. d   16. c   17. d   18. d   19. d   20. b
21. c   22. a   23. b   24. b   25. d   26. b   27. d   28. b   29. a   30. a
31. b   32. d   33. d   34. c   35. b

Chapter 6
1. b   2. d   3. d   4. c   5. d   6. d   7. a   8. a   9. b   10. a
11. b   12. d   13. d   14. a   15. b   16. d   17. d   18. d   19. b   20. a
21. b   22. d   23. d   24. d   25. d   26. c   27. d   28. c   29. d   30. d
31. d

Chapter 7
1. d   2. b   3. b   4. d   5. a   6. a   7. b   8. d   9. d   10. d
11. d   12. a   13. b   14. d   15. d   16. b   17. a   18. d   19. d   20. c
21. a   22. d   23. d   24. d   25. a   26. d   27. d   28. b   29. a   30. c
31. d   32. c   33. d   34. d   35. b   36. d   37. d   38. d   39. d   40. c
41. d   42. d   43. d   44. d   45. a   46. c

Chapter 8
1. d   2. a   3. b   4. b   5. d   6. b   7. a   8. d   9. d   10. a
11. c   12. d   13. b   14. b   15. d   16. c   17. a   18. d   19. c   20. b
21. c   22. d   23. b

ANSWER KEY

Chapter 9
1. a   2. a   3. d   4. c   5. d   6. d   7. d   8. d   9. c   10. d
11. d   12. a   13. d   14. c   15. c   16. d   17. b   18. c   19. d   20. d
21. c   22. d   23. a

Chapter 10
1. b   2. a   3. d   4. d   5. a   6. d   7. d   8. d   9. d   10. d
11. d   12. c   13. d   14. d

Chapter 11
1. d   2. b   3. b   4. d   5. d   6. a   7. d   8. c   9. d   10. d
11. c   12. b   13. a   14. d   15. d   16. d   17. d   18. a   19. d   20. b
21. b   22. c   23. d   24. b   25. d   26. d   27. a   28. d

Chapter 12
1. b   2. d   3. a   4. d   5. d   6. d   7. b   8. d   9. a   10. a
11. d   12. d   13. b   14. d   15. b   16. d   17. a   18. d   19. c   20. d
21. b   22. d   23. b   24. b   25. d   26. c   27. d   28. d   29. c   30. b

Chapter 13
1. b   2. d   3. d   4. d   5. d   6. d   7. b   8. d   9. a   10. d
11. d   12. d   13. d   14. d   15. d   16. b   17. b   18. a   19. d   20. d
21. d   22. d   23. d   24. d   25. c   26. d

Chapter 14
1. b   2. a   3. c   4. a   5. d   6. d   7. c   8. d   9. b   10. d
11. a   12. d   13. d   14. b   15. d   16. d   17. d   18. a   19. d   20. d
21. d   22. d   23. d   24. a   25. d   26. c   27. c   28. b

Chapter 15
1. a   2. d   3. d   4. d   5. a   6. c   7. d   8. d   9. c   10. c
11. b   12. d   13. a   14. d   15. d   16. a   17. d   18. d   19. d   20. c
21. c   22. d   23. c   24. d   25. c   26. d

Chapter 16
1. d   2. d   3. d   4. b   5. b   6. b   7. d   8. a   9. a   10. a
11. c   12. d   13. d   14. d   15. b   16. d   17. d   18. d   19. d

Chapter 17
1. a   2. c   3. b   4. c   5. a   6. a   7. d   8. d   9. b   10. d
11. d   12. d   13. d   14. d   15. d   16. a   17. d   18. d   19. b   20. d
21. b   22. c   23. d   24. a   25. b   26. d   27. d   28. d   29. b   30. c
31. d

Chapter 18

1. b	2. c	3. a	4. d	5. d	6. d	7. d	8. c	9. a	10. d
11. d	12. b	13. d	14. b	15. d					

Chapter 19

1. c	2. a	3. b	4. a	5. d	6. b	7. b	8. b	9. c	10. d
11. c	12. c	13. b	14. c	15. d	16. d	17. a	18. d	19. c	20. d
21. b	22. a	23. d	24. d	25. c	26. d	27. b	28. d	29. d	30. d
31. d	32. d	33. d	34. d	35. d	36. a	37. b			

Chapter 20

1. b	2. b	3. a	4. c	5. d	6. b	7. c	8. d	9. d	10. d
11. d	12. d	13. d	14. d	15. b	16. b	17. c	18. c	19. d	20. d
21. d	22. a	23. d	24. c	25. d	26. d	27. d			

Chapter 21

1. d	2. d	3. b	4. c	5. b	6. d	7. c	8. d	9. d	10. b
11. d	12. a	13. d	14. d	15. d	16. d	17. d	18. d	19. a	20. d
21. d	22. d	23. a	24. a						

Chapter 22

1. b	2. c	3. d	4. b	5. d	6. d	7. c	8. d	9. b	10. d
11. a	12. d	13. b	14. d	15. d	16. c	17. d	18. d	19. d	20. a
21. a	22. c	23. d	24. a	25. d	26. d	27. d	28. a	29. b	30. d
31. c	32. a	33. b	34. d	35. b	36. d	37. c	38. c	39. d	40. a
41. a	42. b	43. d	44. d	45. b	46. d	47. b	48. a	49. d	50. b

www.ingramcontent.com/pod-product-compliance
Lightning Source LLC
Chambersburg PA
CBHW082040230426
43670CB00016B/2726